A NEEDLE

**HOW TO FIND LOVE
IN THE RUBBLE** IN A

HAYSTACK

JAMELIAH GOODEN

The Holy Bible, English Standard Version® (ESV®)
Copyright © 2001 by Crossway,
a publishing ministry of Good News Publishers.
All rights reserved.
ESV Text Edition: 2016

Scripture quotations are from the ESV® Bible.

ISBN: 978-1-954614-71-0 (hard cover)
      978-1-954614-72-7 (soft cover)

Gooden. Jameliah

Edited by: Mary Doyle and Amy Ashby

Published by Warren Publishing
Charlotte, NC
www.warrenpublishing.net
Printed in the United States

INTRODUCTION
A Needle in a Haystack

a needle in a haystack *(noun phrase),* someone or something
that is impossible or extremely difficult to find especially because the
area within which you are searching is too large[1]

I magine you're a farmer in a massive field of hay. You've got to
gather all that hay into bundles, and you've carved a needle out
of wood to get the job done.

There are conflicting accounts about where the phrase *a needle
in a haystack* came from. One of the earliest places the expression
is found in print is in *Don Quixote de la Mancha*, by Miguel de
Cervantes. In part III, chapter 10, the English translation from
Spanish says, "As well look for a needle in a bottle of hay."[2] A
"bottle" of hay is an old-world name for bundle of hay. As early as
the 1600s, people used the term to describe an impossible search.

Now, imagine that scene. You're in a field. You are surrounded
by hay that towers all around you. And what happens? You drop
your wooden needle. You can't just run out to the store and buy
a new needle. You'd have to stop everything and make a new
wooden needle, but you can't afford to stop the reaping to carve
wood. You don't have a choice. You've actually got to dig in there
and find that darn needle. At that point, your search for the needle

might be a bit desperate. You could drive yourself crazy searching for that essential tool, and in all likelihood, the only way you'd find the needle would be through pure luck.

What I love about this description of a needle in a haystack is the way it talks about the vast area you have to search to find your needle. Now, imagine you're back in that field again. You've just lost your needle. You have no idea where to start. It could be anywhere. It feels impossible. You can't help but feel frustrated, and you want to quit before you even get started. You just want to give up.

And that's why we're here. So many people, men and women, gay and straight, Christian or otherwise—we're all out there looking for love. We could say you're looking for love in all the wrong places. What's more likely is that you're looking in an area that is so vast, it feels impossible before you even get started.

———

We're going to focus on exactly where and how you've been searching. Are you looking strictly within your community, perhaps at school, in the clubs (the worst place!), or at church (don't get me started!)? In other words, are you searching the same old places you've always searched? Does that make you feel a bit crazy?

Then, once you meet someone, how do you know if they are worthy of your love? If you've been burned before, how can you prevent that from happening again?

Are you searching alone? Are there people who could be helping you in your search, and once you do find a needle that could be the perfect fit for your needs, are you sabotaging that potential relationship?

We're going to take a hard look at ourselves because searching for the perfect needle is not a solo affair. If you are searching for your needle, there's probably a needle out there searching for you. What work do you need to do to ensure you're found by your perfect fit?

Just like that farmer's field, when you rise up and scan the hayfield, holding your head up over the hay stalks, you realize just how vast the search area can be. It's huge. It's a massive pile of rubble that will make you exhausted just thinking about it. You probably already see it as something that feels impossible, something that will never be achieved, or you wouldn't be reading this book.

So first, you need to understand that what you are looking for is not impossible to find. Then you also need to understand that this search is going to take work. You're going to have to be patient.

We've all been there. You're tired. You're irritated. You've given up. You're to the point where you've convinced yourself that you will never get married. You've convinced yourself that you're going to die alone. Worse, you're so exhausted, you've convinced yourself that you're okay with those outcomes!

It doesn't have to be that way.

As we go through this book, we'll do some exercises to help you figure out where you've been looking and what went wrong. We'll think about what you've done to put yourself out there. Maybe you're afraid to get out there again. Maybe you're recently divorced, or you've just suffered a heartbreak. Maybe the person you just broke up with still has a piece of your heart, and you need something to mend it before you can realize the brightness of your future.

Trust me. I've been in your shoes. I know how hopeless it can feel. I've been divorced, and now I'm here in this new chapter of my life. Since I published my first book, *The Death of the Angry Black Woman* (Warren Publishing, 2018), I have found true love. Love that isn't phony. Love that isn't fake. I found a true, authentic love that I never, ever thought was obtainable for me. I searched through the haystacks and the heaps and the rubble, and I came up with the needle. I found my fit.

Let me tell you, the needle was in the cracks and crevices, in the places you would never expect. The needle you're searching for could be right under your nose but not in your line of sight. The needle could be an old friend, someone close to you. The needle may not be a needle at all.

In my ministry, I have delivered messages to audiences around the world about love and how to find it. Now that I've found my fit, my husband, who is also a minister, we have worked together to share advice in our Couplings seminars, spreading the word about how to find and maintain a relationship—a true partnership—by cultivating the best in each other. We have delivered these seminars on Facebook live and at multiple venues around the country. We are constantly discovering and sharing new insights into love because that is how our love has manifested itself. And now I am delivering some of what we have discovered here.

Hopefully this book will help you see some things through a different set of lenses. Perhaps they are clear lenses that allow you to see that love is obtainable but may not come in the form you thought you were looking for. But what if I told you that you could be digging through that haystack, searching for your needle, and suddenly, you wind up pricking yourself on something you weren't even expecting?

We're going to turn the pages of this book and examine every layer of love. Hopefully, by the time we get to the end, you'll understand why I've called it *A Needle in a Haystack*.

As you turn these pages, we will examine:
- what you are looking for;
- the difference between standards and settling;
- how to gather the data you need to make wise choices;
- what your red flags are and why you keep ignoring them;
- how to identify the qualities within yourself that are worth finding;
- how to find help in your search;
- how to know when you've found The Real Thing (TRT).

I'm sure you're going to find things within these pages that will speak to you. I suggest you grab a pen, make some notes in the margins, or scribble concepts down on paper. I'll be giving you some assignments to get you thinking. You might also want to get a couple of friends in your same situation to read the book as well. Believe me. It will help you to discuss some of the concepts with the people closest to you. More discovery will come when you exchange some ideas about what you could all do differently to enhance the search for your perfect fit.

When we talk about searching for true love, we often think it's just women who are doing the searching. That's not true. I've written these pages for both women and men. The concepts are about understanding what you are looking for, being ready for it, and being successful in your search. These are concepts and needs that cross all boundaries.

Yes, I'm here to help you understand that somewhere in that haystack, there *is* a needle waiting to find you.

So are you ready for this? Let's go.

CHAPTER ONE
The Heap

heap (ˈhēp), **noun,** advanced data structure
that is engaged for specific usages; cases such
as sorting, implementing, or prioritizing[3]

I know it sounds funny, but I want you to try to think of your relationship search as if you are digging through *heaps* as they are defined above.

In the search for love, most people will look in the same old places they've always looked. You put on your best face, gather a group of friends, and head out for a night on the town. You tell yourself you're just there for a fun night out, but if you're single and you're hoping to find someone special to spend the rest of your life with, you're also there to look.

Have you noticed that women always outnumber men in the clubs? By a lot! And when it comes to African American women, the odds are much worse. The single women always outnumber the single men by what feels like three or four to one. And if you're out with a group of friends, chances are, every one of you is gunning for the same man. It's unfortunate, but you know it's true.

Maybe, instead of going to clubs, you're using social media or online chat groups to meet that special someone. Or you put together a flattering profile and have ventured into the online dating sites. Don't get me wrong—I'm not discrediting these types of searches. A lot of people have found love with online dating or other technologies.

And of course, there's church. You're always in church. You know everybody at church. They're your family and you feel safe there. If you see someone new in your house of worship, you know your church family can always give you the lowdown. Church is a safe space. But just like in the club, everyone has their eye on the same man. Now you're left to figure out how to get his attention. Should you be bold and aggressive? Find some way to draw attention to yourself? The things we do to try to get the right set of eyes to swing our way don't always leave us with the dignity we deserve.

Statistically, men are much more likely to find the relationships they're looking for because they have so many more choices. The fact is: The odds are against us, especially for Black women.[4] Why is that?

It feels even harder for black women because we're all gathering data from the same database. We're all going to the same clubs, the same church, doing the same old things we always do, day after day, time after time. Does it make you feel crazy? Sure it does because insanity is when you do the same thing over and over and expect a different result.

At the beginning of this chapter, we started with a definition of "heap." Heaps are a way to sort and prioritize data. And the truth is, you've been searching that same heap, that same database, and coming up empty. No matter how you sort or prioritize the data you find, the solution simply isn't there. And if you keep searching the same database, you end up with a heap of confusion, a heap of frustration. You can chase after a party or club or dating website or take singles vacations over and over. The results are still the same.

By this point, most people are just done. They've searched their heap, they've calculated the data, the solution is never found, so they give up.

It does not work.

You need to step out of that environment, come out of your routine. You need to think about where you go to meet people

SEE THE WORKBOOK AT THE END OF THIS CHAPTER TO EXAMINE WHERE YOU GO TO MEET PEOPLE. THE EXERCISE WILL ASK YOU TO RATE THE LOCATIONS IN ORDER OF PREFERENCE.

and why meeting someone is so prominent in your mind when you go to those places.

I'm going to keep saying this because we know it's true. Women are competitive. We go to a club where everyone is attracted to the same man, and because you're competing with all the other women in your heap, you try harder. It becomes a competition. When it's a competition, someone wins and someone loses, and none of us want to lose.

YOU NEED TO CHANGE YOUR DATABASE.

So how do we fix this? What if I told you that you've been searching the wrong database? You're looking for a solution in the database that's familiar. You think if you just keep looking, you'll find that needle in the haystack, but the truth is, you've been searching the wrong haystack all along.

I'm not single anymore, but I understand what it is to be single. I know that the familiar heaps are the places you walk into with an expectation. You go to church with an expectation. You go to the mall with an expectation. You get dressed beforehand with an expectation in mind.

> "IF YOU EXPECT NOTHING FROM SOMEBODY
> YOU ARE NEVER DISAPPOINTED."
> —SYLVIA PLATH[5]

For a start, remind yourself that dating is meant to be fun. Dating is not a search for a husband. A first date is not when you should be thinking about the possibility of marriage. Dating is a chance to share a meal, have fun, and enjoy the company of the person you are with. If a second date comes out of it, that's a bonus. If not, you had an enjoyable evening with someone new. You've gathered the data you need.

When you let go of your competitive notions, when you relax and enjoy the evening instead of allowing your expectations to get the better of you, you give off a very different vibe. It becomes noticeable for someone who just wants to enjoy a night out. It's an attitude that is attractive because you're not prioritizing or competing; you're just having a good time, doing whatever it is you are doing. You are in the moment, and that is naturally attractive.

If you're searching in a haystack, you at least need to make sure it's the right heap, right? If you relax, stay in the moment, and enjoy a date for what it is, that pile of hay won't feel as vast.

———

Now, I want you to think of the heap like a pile of leaves. If you're a kid, and you've lost something in that pile, you could be panicked because you're afraid you'll never find what you've lost.

On the other hand, if you're a kid and you haven't lost anything, you've simply found a big pile of leaves. To a child, a big pile of leaves looks like nothing but fun. What are you going to do? You're going to throw yourself into it and play, throwing leaves in the air and experiencing the joy of being a kid in a pile of leaves!

DON'T TRY TO CONTROL THE HEAP, OR THE HEAP WILL CONTROL YOU.

The heap is a big, colossal mess of stuff, people, personalities, colors, and ethnic backgrounds, and you need to learn to enjoy all of it for what it is without an expectation. Learn to enjoy yourself. Enjoy the camaraderie. The change in your energy will mean that good experiences will be drawn to you. I guarantee you, dating will become fun again.

The next couple of pages are the first in your haystack workbook. Take your time with the assignments. I suggest you revisit them multiple times as you progress and make note of the evolution of your ideas and approaches.

WHAT KIND OF NEEDLE
ARE YOU LOOKING FOR?

It's time to begin your list. What **characteristics** does your needle have? What aspects of **appearance** are you looking for in your needle? You may want to complete this list in pencil. This is a living document. As you work your way through this book, you may find that different things will become more important to you. Be open to changes.

Characteristics	Appearance
Shares my religious beliefs	Taller than me
Honest and open	Concerned with health
Serious but willing to laugh	and wellness

LOCATION, LOCATION, LOCATION!

Think about the locations you enter with an expectation of meeting a potential mate. Have you ever met a potential date in these locations? Circle the ones that apply and feel free to add your own.

Church   Online dating service
Weddings   Grocery store
Gym/workout/yoga class   Blind dates/dinner parties
School/class   Workplace/conferences
Parties/barbeques   Night club/dance club
Neighborhood park/dog park   PTA/parents' meetings

Locations not listed above:

Have you listed any place that you think you should take off your list? Do you see any problems with relying on any of these locations for finding your needle?

NEW LOCATIONS?

You've listed your usual haunts. What new locations should you consider? Create a list of potential places below.

Example: Exotic locations like Tahiti, Belize, etc.

CHAPTER TWO
What Is Your Worth?

ruby ('rü-bē), *noun,* a precious stone that is a red corundum;
something (such as a watch bearing) made of ruby;
the dark red color of the ruby; something resembling a ruby in color[6]

M y grandfather was a West Virginia coal miner. Yes, I am a coal miner's granddaughter!

By the time I was old enough to remember, he was no longer going to the mines but still maintained the habit of leaving his shoes outside the door. I saw plenty of pictures that showed how he looked when he came home from a day of working thousands of feet beneath the earth. He was covered in coal dust, his face and clothes black with it. He wore a hard hat with a headlamp, and his hands were bloody at times from wielding a pickax or scrambling at rocks. His eyes were bloodshot and teary from the dust. All you had to do was look at the pictures—him standing there, filthy from head to toe and surrounded by a group of fellow workers covered in dust—and you could clearly see that coal mining was backbreaking, relentless, and dangerous work.

No matter how difficult it was, he would go to work each day under tons of earth to dig for precious lumps of coal. My mother told me she and my grandmother would run to him when he came home, appreciative of the backbreaking work he performed to keep food on the table and a roof over their heads.

Coal mining is not for the faint at heart. Thousands of people have lost their lives digging into the fissures of the earth to find the precious fuel.

Why am I telling you all this?

Because anything of value or substance is going to be hidden from view. It may not be as deeply buried as coal, nor should obtaining it be as dangerous or as backbreaking, but you will need determination and resilience for this search if you're to find a relationship that will stand the test of time.

If you could walk along the road and fill a basket full of coal, what kind of value would you assign to it? When we talk about precious metals or precious gems, we label them as such because they are rare or hard to find.

The scripture says, "Who can find a virtuous woman? For her value is far more than rubies" (Proverbs 31:10 ESV).[7]

I travel quite a bit doing conferences, and I speak to a lot of people seeking love, people who are searching for their fit. No matter whom I speak to, whether it be men or women, they all share something in common: they all want to be found. No one— trust me on this—no one wants to be lonely. For some, the search is too arduous, perhaps too much like the backbreaking work of coal mining. They grow tired of the search and give up. Since you're reading this book, I know you haven't given up yet, and you shouldn't. Stick with me and, hopefully, I can give you some tools to make the work less like drudgery and more like discovery.

> MAKE THE WORK OF FINDING YOUR NEEDLE LESS
> LIKE DRUDGERY AND MORE LIKE DISCOVERY.

Now, back to Proverbs 31. The scripture talks about rubies. It says if you can get your hands on a ruby, you have found something precious. We need to understand that we are like those rubies. Every one of us has a level of value. It's so unfortunate when people find themselves in relationships with someone who doesn't have an appreciation of their worth. Don't let that be you.

> "IT IS SO LIBERATING TO REALLY KNOW WHAT I WANT, WHAT TRULY MAKES ME HAPPY, WHAT I WILL NOT TOLERATE. I HAVE LEARNED THAT IT IS NO ONE ELSE'S JOB TO TAKE CARE OF ME BUT ME."
> —BEYONCÉ KNOWLES[8]

I'm gonna say it again. Everyone has value. What you need to do in your search is find someone who appreciates you for you, appraises you correctly, and understands your worth.

When my grandfather was digging for coal, he would travel thousands of feet beneath the earth to bring up the needed fuel that powered towns and cities and kept his family fed. When miners search for rubies, they may dig into rock using pickaxes or even explosives to break up the rubble. They might pan for rubies with water and a shallow tray, just as panning for gold is done, sifting through mounds of rock, waiting for the tiny, precious rubies to rise to the top of the worthless sediment. That's often what you have to do when you're searching for these precious things found in the crevices of the earth.

To find something of value, you need to dig, and that means you need to bring a level of strength and resilience to the search because this will not be easy. When my grandfather came out of the mines, he looked like he had been through something

YOU ALSO NEED TO HAVE SOME KNOWLEDGE, SOME FAITH, IF YOU WILL, THAT YOU ARE LOOKING IN THE RIGHT PLACE. ARE YOU GOING TO INVEST THE TIME AND BACKBREAKING ENERGY TO DIG INTO THE EARTH IF THERE'S A CHANCE YOU'RE NOT GOING TO END UP WITH A RUBY?

unimaginable with his bloody hands, bloodshot eyes, and coal-covered face. That should be a clue to you. If you want to find your precious gem, you are going to need to go through some things.

There may be breakups. There may be makeups. You may have your hopes dashed and need to start all over. That's because what is worth searching for is valuable, and this might mean you'll need to fight for it. You may get knocked around a bit in the process, but you're a fighter, or you wouldn't be here now.

———

My grandfather must have been a fighter. I sometimes wonder how he could get up each day, get dressed, and go down into that mine, knowing how dark and awful and dangerous it would be. He did it because he loved his family; he loved his wife. They were married for almost sixty years before they both passed. My grandparents married when they were fifteen years old in a ceremony that took place under a tree outside of my Aunt Claire's house. Can you imagine that? Fifteen years old. So I grew up hearing about the example of love and endurance they set. It's an example I will never forget.

ACCORDING TO A MATCH.COM SURVEY, RELEASED FEB. 4, 2011, 54 PERCENT OF MEN SAY THEY HAVE EXPERIENCED LOVE AT FIRST SIGHT COMPARED TO 44 PERCENT OF WOMEN. FORTY-THREE PERCENT OF SINGLES FELL IN LOVE WITH SOMEONE THEY INITIALLY DID NOT FIND ATTRACTIVE OR FELL IN LOVE AFTER BECOMING BEST FRIENDS.[9]

Some people seem to find love in a minute. After a first date, they may be confident in the knowledge that they have found their fit. My husband says he knew he was looking at his wife the moment he saw me. That melts my heart every time I think of it, but the reality is, that instant knowledge will not happen for everyone. Also, while they might say they knew instantly, you don't know what kind of struggle they went through digging, mining, and searching for you before that instant. You also don't know what kind of struggle they may have ahead of them because even as you find your true love, you will need to do work on that relationship and work on the people around you to ensure they are ready for the love you will be sharing.

What would have happened had my grandfather decided his job was just too hard? What would have happened had he decided he was not going to spend another day down in that mine? What if he had complained that his hands were bloody, that he couldn't take another day with soot in his eyes, or that he didn't want to be covered from head to foot in coal dust? Who could have blamed him?

What makes me sad is when people tell me they've given up their search because they're tired. They've had enough. "I'm done," they say. "This means nothing to me anymore. I'm past my childbearing years. I'm too old for this." Even people who are widowed or have lost love in some other way may stop digging, either because they've lost interest, or they don't see the value in finding love anymore.

When you understand the value of love, of what it means to have love, you will pay the price for it. The value you assign to it should be equal to the effort you are willing to put toward finding it.

So how bad do you want it?

I hear so many women say they want to be married by a particular age, that they want to have three children and a house and a vacation home. They have all these expectations and timelines they've tied to their dreams. When things don't shake out the way they've planned, or if their timeline is overcome by events, they get discouraged and give up.

Essentially, they are saying "I'm not valuable enough to be found. I'm not worth further effort." By making such choices, they sometimes stop working on themselves and give up hope. They stop working toward anyone else finding them. Or maybe some breakup was so bad that the bitterness has become like the soot of coal dust. It leaves you feeling bloody, and your eyes hurt, and you're tired of going down into that pit and just want to give up. The pain of that breakup has camouflaged your worth so well, you are more difficult to find because your brightness is diminished.

Part of the work you need to do is understanding your worth and truly believing in your value. You need to believe, even through your pain, that you are worthy of love. You need to believe in your value enough that even if you are buried beneath the rubble of a painful breakup or stumbling through the debris of your shattered timeline, you still have the fight and the resilience to wipe yourself off and stay in the fight.

You also need to believe that, just as my grandfather and grandmother did, someone will look past the soot, the bloody hands, and the bloodshot eyes and see your value, believe in your worth, and decide to love you. Consider this question: How will they find and believe in that value if you don't believe in it yourself?

That's the beauty of a ruby. A ruby understands its value. It doesn't have to work to be beautiful. It just is, and it doesn't have to do anything to convince anyone of that. The person who goes searching for the ruby will go to great lengths, spending days and weeks sifting through rubble to find that gem and make it their own.

When you manage to find that shimmer in yourself, it will shine for someone else to find. Even through all the stuff you've been through, the pain, heartache, frustration, and fear of failure, someone will see that glimmer in you. Because we like shiny things, don't we?

It happened to me.

It can happen for you too, and it begins with understanding that you are worth digging for. Remember: If you can't judge your own value, if you don't appraise yourself to be worthy of the love you seek, how will your worth appear to someone else?

WHAT IS YOUR WORTH?

What qualities and values do you bring to a relationship? Without fixating on physical aspects or bank balances, what aspects of your personality or character bring value to a relationship?

Example: I enjoy trying new things.

What improvements can you make to ensure your perfect needle can find you?

Example: I would like to read more to broaden my worldview.

CHAPTER THREE
The Search

discovery (di-'skə-v(ə-)rē, *noun*, the action or process
of discovering; something discovered[10]

When I was a kid, my mother used to organize the annual Easter egg hunt for our Sunday school. She would go to Prospect Park and scatter the colorful, hard-boiled eggs in the grass. The egg hunt was so exciting. We would go screaming into that field, eager to get caught up in the search. A prize was given to the child who found the most eggs, so the search itself was the game.

Do you remember the joy a searching game gave you? Easter egg hunts, scavenger hunts, hide-and-go-seek—those games of our youth were all about the pleasure of finding something before anyone else did. The incentive was to win by discovering the coveted goal at the end.

As adults, every day, we are constantly searching for things, but the joy we felt as children is missing. We search for the right job, the right career, the right hair stylist, a good deal on a major purchase. We search for the right pair of shoes to match that outfit we've had in the closet forever. We search for apartments or houses, the best car, or the right hotel for our next vacation. The number of times you open a search engine in a day is just a glimpse of how often you're on the hunt for something.

Right now, I am so exhausted. I'm preparing for a family vacation, and I've spent the entire day running around, searching for the things we need to take with us. The pleasure this trip will bring to my family alone should be my incentive, but it's still exhausting. All day long, I've been searching for things, and let me tell you, I am tired of looking.

The truth is, when you've been searching for a long time, you start to forget what you're looking for in the first place. You lose the incentive you had when you began your search. You're left with the painful frustration and belief that you will never find what you're looking for. You just want to give up.

THE DATING GAME, 1965–1986: CREATED BY CHUCK BARRIS. WITHOUT SEEING THEM, A SINGLE WOMAN CHOOSES ONE OF THREE BACHELORS AFTER ASKING THEM A SERIES OF QUESTIONS. THE BACHELOR SELECTED IS THE WINNER, AND THE TWO GO ON A DATE TOGETHER.[11]

When you lose the incentive, continuing begins to feel fruitless—a big game you've grown tired of playing. Maybe that's why they call it *The Dating Game*. Whatever you call it, if you keep coming up empty no matter where you look, you start to feel as if you're on the losing end of the proposition. You're playing a game of cat and mouse that is doomed to fail.

Does any of this sound familiar? You're staying up at night searching the internet, going on website after website, and combing social media, hoping that somewhere, somehow, you'll make a connection that will give your mind, body, and heart some rest.

Are you ready for this? You improve your chances of finding love by leveling the heap and clearing away the excess rubble. And the best way to clear that rubble away is by starting the search within yourself. You need to search for that thing inside yourself that will connect you to someone who is waiting to be found.

It's like that Easter egg hunt. What if you didn't know what an egg looked like? You're standing on a field filled with eggs being told to go search for an egg, yet you have no way of recognizing it. Once someone shows you the egg—or in the case of dating, once you recognize the thing inside yourself that exemplifies what you're looking for—it becomes much easier to find an egg to match it.

I'll get back to that in a minute.

Sifting through the rubble takes time, and time is one of the only things God gave you that you are allowed to give to someone else. You can't control time, but you can give it. Whatever you are searching for will require your time. Give it wisely, because you're going to need quite a bit of it.

———

It took me years before I stumbled across the man I now call my husband. It took a few tries, a lot of tears, and an emotional investment to learn which men weren't right for me. There were times when I told myself I didn't want to search anymore. It wasn't until I gave myself permission to devote some time in myself—to figure out what I needed and what I had to offer—that what I was searching for found me because he was searching too.

Have you ever watched the cartoon *An American Tail?* One of the characters is Fievel Mousekewitz—he's a mouse, by the way. He sang "Somewhere Out There." It was a song I'd heard before, but when he sings in his little mousey voice about being underneath the same sky with someone you have yet to meet, it stuck with me.[12]

In other words, not only is your future partner under the same blue sky, they are also on the same search you are.

Looking in the right places is important. Where do people find love? According to a 2017 study by ReportLinker, a technology-based research service, 39 percent of people cited friends as the source for meeting their love interest. Others cited work (15 percent); bars, coffee shops, or public areas (12 percent); religion or hobby (9 percent); internet app (8 percent); family (7 percent); school (6 percent); or other, including speed-dating events (4 percent).[13]

Meeting that special someone is going to take time. Take some of that time to search inside yourself. Understand what it is you are offering because, believe it or not, someone is searching for you too. Anything worth finding in someone else is even more worth finding inside yourself. If you are taking the time to scramble over the heap, looking for a characteristic that is important to you, it's probably important to the person you are searching for as well. Is what you're searching for inside yourself?

I told you that I'm exhausted today because I've been running around looking for things my family needs for our upcoming trip. It's very much like your search. Yes, it's exhausting. My incentive for continuing my search is the joy I know I will see on the faces of my family when we are on our trip and have everything we need. That joy will make my search worth it.

YOUR SEARCH BEACON

Let's build on the last exercise. You've looked at what things of value you bring to a relationship. You've also thought about ways you can improve your value.

What values or characteristics are you looking for in your needle? Are those same values found within yourself?

CHAPTER FOUR
Pitfalls of Dating

We all know people who are a bit obsessed with some things. Maybe they spend every waking moment watching sports or playing video games. Maybe they have shelves full of cookbooks, or they collect toy cars or dolls. Maybe you know someone who is constantly cleaning and straightening things, preoccupied to the point of distraction with everything being in exactly the right place.

People can obsess about a lot of things, and there are some people who are addicted to searching for their needle. I'm going to go so far as to call them "needle freaks."

What I'm talking about are people who are addicted to gathering needles. They don't care if the needles are too long or short. They don't care if the needles are rusted or shiny. Even when they know the needles aren't right for them, they don't care. Like someone who collects toy cars or dolls, they just want to fill their life with needles.

Losing the metaphor, these are folks who like the thrill of going to dinner, meeting someone new, and sitting across from someone who is interested in what they have to say. They like the first blush of a relationship and will hang around just long enough for that blush to wear off. And yes, some like to skip the date and go straight to the hookup.

In an article in *Women's Health Magazine*, Helen Fisher, PhD, a biological anthropologist and the chief scientific advisor for Match.com, says it's only logical that some people will be addicted to dating. "Looking for love is the most important thing we do in our lives," said Fisher. "You're trying to win love's greatest prize, a mating partner. I'm not surprised that people become addicted to trying."[15]

ACCORDING TO *WOMEN'S HEALTH MAGAZINE* AND A STUDY BY SINGLES IN AMERICA WITH MATCH.COM, DATING ADDICTION IS REAL AND MOST PREVALENT IN MILLENNIALS. WHEN COMPARED TO OLDER GENERATIONS, MILLENNIALS WHO SELF-DESCRIBE AS BEING ADDICTED TO GOING ON DATES WITH NEW PEOPLE ARE 125 PERCENT MORE LIKELY TO DO SO.[14]

I don't care if you're twenty-five, fifty-five, or one hundred and five, some people are hooked on the jolt they get when meeting new people, especially in a romantic setting.

We just talked about the search and how the thrill of finding something can be rewarding. We make games out of it because finding the things we're looking for makes us feel like winners. Long, drawn-out searches—without the thrill of finding what you want—are exhausting and frustrating. Isn't it much more satisfying to search and convince yourself that you've found that special something over and over again?

There are those who enjoy the rush of sifting through the rubble and meeting new people, but in their hearts, they have no intention of establishing anything serious with anyone. They just want to keep looking. They want to continue the search.

This is not a man thing. It's not a woman thing. I am labeling this a people thing. When you're addicted to the needle, there's always joy in the new find. If this is you, you need to be honest about it. Admit to yourself that you're not serious about finding an everlasting, true love. Once you're honest with yourself about what you really want, be sure to also be honest with the people you date.

"I'm not looking for love. I just enjoy the journey and getting to know new people." Say it to yourself. Say it to your date.

This honesty about what you are searching for is even more important when sex is involved. Some people are addicted to the thrill of that first night of sex. Some are addicted to what they think is uncomplicated sex. And some are addicted to the thrill of meeting someone and having an evening of connection during which they say and do all the right things and overwhelm their date with the romance and the thrill. One partner thinks there is an incredibly magical night going on, while the other is making it magical because they've had so much practice doing it. In reality, they have no intention of continuing with the work and effort it takes to develop a relationship.

That kind of emotional manipulation is soul crushing and wrong.

If you're one of those people addicted to the search, imagine yourself on the other side of the table. Imagine thinking you've found someone special after a long and hard search. Then imagine the overwhelming realization that it was not at all what you thought it would be.

This book is about finding a needle in a haystack, but it doesn't stop there. It's about finding true love and keeping it. People who are addicted to the search are not keepers. They are serial daters.

It's very much like that person you know who has been going to school their entire life and never seems to graduate. Some will get to a point in their education journey and then switch majors and start all over again. It's as if they fear what will happen when they finally have a degree and have to follow it with a career in whatever field they studied. They love to study. They love learning new things. There is nothing wrong with either of those things, but there is something wrong with avoiding the next phase.

There are all kinds of crazy addictions in the world, and trust me, addiction to dating is real. The danger, of course, is that you will get caught up in someone else's addiction and have no idea until it's too late that your date isn't serious about you. The serial dater doesn't ever want to get married or commit. The worst part is, they're looking for someone just like you who is serious about finding love because you are the most vulnerable.

Imagine a real needle, not the metaphorical kind. You thread it, you sew something together, but you don't do it properly. The stitches are weak. There are holes in your work. Eventually, it's all going to come apart. In the end, you're left with ragged pieces that don't resemble what you were trying to make.

Now I've already said if you're addicted to the thrill of the find, you need to be honest with yourself and honest with anyone you date. You also need to be honest if you're someone who is repeatedly taken in by serial daters. Are you making the mistake of dating people who aren't serious? Are you attracted to people who come on fast and strong right away?

Learning who someone really is takes time. If the person you are dating is professing love on the first or second date, it might be thrilling, but it might also be dangerous to you and your heart. If you never get to the part when you're actually learning who the real person is behind the heart-pounding thrill, you might be addicted to dating.

Dating should be fun. Dating should bring you pleasure, but if both people aren't on the date for the same reasons, dating can lead to heartache. And heartache can lead to some serious emotional issues. When you invest your heart in a relationship with someone who never had the intention of building something real, the self-recriminations can be crippling. Many addictions can be hurtful to the people who operate around the addicted person. Getting pulled into a relationship with someone who isn't serious, means someone will pay with their heart. Invest your heart wisely.

How do you protect yourself from a serial dater? The next chapter will offer you a bit of dating advice, specifically about gathering the data you need to make a true assessment of the person who has sparked your interest. When it comes to addiction, you might want to know how many dates this person has been on in the previous six months. What do you know about the patterns they've had with previous relationships? Sometimes history will reveal whether this is someone who likes to dig through the haystack, only to throw the needles they've found back into the pile.

Going on multiple dates in a short amount of time doesn't automatically mean someone is addicted. People have many reasons for dating. It's your job to date with an eye on safety. You may discover your date has a purpose and a plan you don't want to be a part of.

I love meeting new people and get a rush when I'm connecting with someone new. It might be a doctor one day, an attorney the next, the barista at the local coffee shop, or the clerk at the grocery store the following day. People who are addicted to finding the needle take the thrill of meeting new people to a whole other level. There is a healthy way to meet new people, and then there is an unhealthy, manipulative way that can ultimately result in someone getting hurt.

There is also the possibility that you will read this chapter and recognize yourself. If the thrill of finding your needle is only about that, the thrill, you might want to seek help. A big part of this journey is learning about yourself and making the kinds of adjustments that make you someone who is worthy of being found. I am a firm believer that everyone can benefit from therapy. If you suspect you're addicted to the thrill of finding a needle, discussing it with a professional might be a good idea for you.

CHAPTER FIVE
Gathering Data

When someone shows you who they are, believe them the first time. People know themselves much better than you do. That's why it's important to stop expecting them to be something other than who they are.

—Maya Angelou[16]

Girl, I'm just gonna say it. Eat them wings and shut up! You may think that sounds rude or harsh. When someone tells you to shut up, you may want to respond with the same derogatory tone in which the comment was made. This is no time to be polite. I need you to listen.

Eat them wings and shut up. I mean it.

Because a date is not a free meal. A date is not a chance to order the most expensive item on the menu. A date is not a confessional for you to pour your heart out and share all your business with someone.

A date, especially one that happens early on, is a chance to gather data. You cannot gather data if you are running your mouth!

Let me tell you what happens. You're sitting across the table from this person. You're nervous or just trying to make conversation. You may be struggling with what to say. You decide you just want to be honest about exactly what you're looking for because this honesty, you feel, will somehow make your search easier.

It won't. It will make your search harder. Let me tell you why.

When you start running your mouth, you practically read directly from your list of perfect-mate attributes. Men, I want you to take this next part in because women are very prone to doing this sort of thing.

You've told your date exactly what you are looking for and why. So what does that other person do? They listen to those ingredients and present themselves in a way that most closely represents your list. You want soft-spoken? Sophisticated? A father for your child or a woman who will support your wish to have alone time when you need it? You want someone interested in the same hobby you are?

Like magic, they become exactly what you've been searching for. You've found your fit, right?

Wrong.

> LIKE IT OR NOT, YOU HAVE TO UNDERSTAND THAT NOT EVERYONE IS AS INTERESTED AND AS DEDICATED TO FINDING A LIFE PARTNER AS YOU MAY BE.

They may have their own reasons for becoming the mirror image of the person you describe, but whatever the reason, they are not what they represent. They've listened to the recipe you've given them and used it to serve themselves up as the perfect dish.

More importantly, you may talk about what it is you're looking for at the same time you talk about how unsuccessful you've been. Instead of commiserating with you about your unsuccessful search, the other person only sees your vulnerability. They see the desperation in your eyes. They see the need you don't even know you are broadcasting. It becomes easy for them to convince you that they are the answer to your prayers.

Eat them wings and shut up!

Stop talking so much. Instead of talking, listen. This is not just a dinner date. This is an opportunity to gather data. In fact, your rule should be that you won't pass on any data on your first date. A first date is for gathering data, not giving all of yours away.

A date is a chance to get to know someone and gather that data to determine whether or not this person is dinner-worthy, bowling-worthy, boyfriend- or girlfriend-worthy, friendship-worthy, Netflix-and-chill-worthy ... with your clothes *on*, of course!

You need to allow this person the room and space to tell you who they are. If you reveal too much about what you're looking for, or if you somehow convey the loneliness, pain, and perhaps the desperation you feel, you may ruin your opportunity to gather the true, uninfluenced data you need to make a clear judgment about whether or not this person is right for you. You'll miss the realness and the window of opportunity to amass that clean data.

If you can be quiet and enjoy the moment for what it is, you can learn so much. Whether that's dinner or a movie or both, or you're just sitting together and chilling— be in the moment.

Hopefully, when you are with your friends, you feel very comfortable, but no matter how close you all are now, you didn't become friends overnight. Rome wasn't built in a day, and neither will any relationship be.

One thing is for sure. If you keep talking and revealing the structure, the cornerstone, the foundation, the rooftop, the doorknob, and the frame, you've built an entire

ACCORDING TO A SINGLES IN AMERICA STUDY, THE COVID-19 LOCKDOWN WAS GOOD FOR DATING. SIXTY-THREE PERCENT OF SINGLES SAID THEY SPENT MORE TIME GETTING TO KNOW THEIR POTENTIAL PARTNERS; 59 PERCENT SAID THEY CONSIDERED A WIDER RANGE OF PARTNERS. 50 PERCENT SAID THEY NEEDED MORE MEANINGFUL CONVERSATION BEFORE MEETING IN PERSON. IN BALTIMORE, 94 PERCENT OF APP DATERS SAID THEY WERE MORE LIKELY TO ASK A DATE WHAT KIND OF RELATIONSHIP THEY WERE LOOKING FOR.[17]

structure—and given enough information for someone else to enter into that house even if it hasn't been built with enough stability to hold a person. It's dangerous to be on a date and say, "I'm looking for a husband," "I'm looking for a wife," or "I want to get married." If you're talking like that from the doorway of this structure you've built, you need to be very careful.

I'm going to say this. A lot of men may not like what I'm about to say, but it's the truth. If a woman says she's looking for a husband, 90 percent of the men are going to run the other way. When a man says he's looking for a wife—and I can't stand it when they do this—he knows exactly what kind of reaction he's going to get. How many women are out there looking for a husband? How many would take the extra effort to attract the man who has stated in clear terms that he's looking for a wife? Some of them may actually be looking for matrimony. Unfortunately, a number of them are simply looking to prey on women who have stated their desire for marriage.

If they are the type, knowledge of your vulnerability is an invitation for manipulation. You make yourself a target when you talk too much about what you want. Instead of eating your wings and enjoying the blue cheese and the hot sauce, you go on a tangent. Your biological clock is ticking, your heart has been broken before, you've reached a place of desperation, you have your list, you're looking at everyone around you, and you can't enjoy what you're doing in the moment.

You need to drop the expectations you've had in the past regarding the dating process. Instead of dating with the idea that you will find your potential soul mate, date with the expectation of finding a friend. Then, if something else happens, it will happen over the course of time.

My husband said he knew I was his wife the moment he saw my face. Sometimes, it happens that way. But to find your fit, you have to be patient. When it happens, it is spiritual—your fit is everything. Ecclesiastes says it would be:

> Two are better than one, because they have a good
> reward for their toil. For if they fall, one will lift up
> his fellow. But woe to him who is alone when he
> falls and has not another to lift him up! Again, if

two lie together, they keep warm, but how can one keep warm alone? And though a man might prevail against one who is alone, two will withstand him—a threefold cord is not quickly broken. (Ecclesiastes 4:9–12, ESV)[18]

Finding your needle is not something that will happen overnight. It's not like the *Jerry McGuire* movie where love happens at hello. Don't expect love to hit you while you're still on the appetizer and to move on to marriage before you get to the main course.

Love happens over the course of time because the emotion needs to be built, just like anything else. It takes time and energy. When you do find your fit, you will realize that individual is someone who is willing to do the work with you and go through the pain with you.

You may be like my husband when he said he knew the moment he saw me. You may feel that immediate connection, but some fits are going to take time.

You know this already, but instead of eating the wings, you rush to the main course, and then you think, *This is the person I want.* But the person you think you want may not be the person actually sitting across from you at that dinner table.

Now, here's some truth. And this is for men and women. I want you both to pay attention. Instead of eating them wings and shutting up, instead of having a cold beer or a cognac or whatever you're drinking at the time (I'm not judging; you can have a drink in moderation while you're gathering data), instead of allowing yourself to be friend-worthy, he picks up on your vulnerability, looks at you, and thinks, *I can get everything I want from her because she's letting me know from the gate she's looking for something. So I'm going to be that individual she's looking for.* In his mind, he sees your vulnerability. You've presented an opportunity for him to use you.

Don't get me wrong. Not everyone is like that. But you have to admit, there are people out there who are very good at the game, and it's the game that makes you tired, that makes you want to give up the search.

But consider this. Have you ever thought that you are the one who is playing the game? Is it possible you've come out on the losing end because you've put all your pieces on the board, giving your date every opportunity to find a means to win the game and get his checkmate? Let me tell you—you lost that game because you didn't eat them wings and stay quiet and gather your data!

Most people will show their true nature when they're in a happy, healthy, friendly environment. You throw stress into that mix when you start sharing the list that defines your perfect partner. If you talk about all the things you want and stay fixated on checking qualities off your list, you won't even notice that your date already has one foot out the door. After all, the person sitting across from you thought they were just going on a date. They aren't sure if they're ready for all the boxes you're asking them to check.

If you eat them wings and shut up, trust that you will project the image of your true self. You've made your list or are currently working on it. You've identified the things you want to find in a partner, and, in the process, you've identified the things within yourself you hold valuable, the things you want your date to see in you. And by not giving potential partners a list of criteria to meet, you instead give them time to become a friend. Even if the date doesn't work out, perhaps you've still made a solid companion. If you have a good friendship, it's possible the two of you may develop a good relationship later. This may sound harsh. Telling you not to appear desperate doesn't seem nice. Telling you to shut up and eat them wings is not nice either, but as I've learned, thanks to what God has taught me, it's better to hurt your feelings and save your life than let you drown. Before you make another mistake, I'm gonna give you the hard truth, and that is, you need to eat the damn wings and shut up!

BEST DATA-MINING LOCATIONS

We've talked about the expectations you might have to meet a potential needle when you go to certain locations (see Location, Location, Location).

Now, let's consider that location is important to the success of a first date. The saying goes, not all relationships lead to marriage. Some will help you discover new restaurants!

A good first-date location offers good data-mining opportunities. Think about your most successful first dates. Where did they take place, and why were they successful? Think beyond restaurants and consider locations or activities that might spark conversation or reveal aspects of your date's personality.

Example: A Japanese hibachi restaurant—because the food is good, and it's fun to see how your date may interact with the strangers at the table.

CHAPTER SIX
To Settle

settle ('se-təl), *transitive verb,* to make quiet
or orderly; to fix or resolve conclusively;
to establish or secure permanently[19]

When people make bad relationship or dating decisions, they often say they settled, meaning they made a choice or a decision because what they really wanted wasn't available. They blame the unsuccessful relationship on the idea that they settled for something less desirable than what they were originally searching for.

First off, understand that there is a big difference between settling and choosing someone who doesn't meet your standards. We will cover standards and compromising those standards in the next chapter. For now, let's come to an understanding of what it means when we talk about settling.

You should already have or should be working on a list of characteristics you would love to find in your partner. Remember, this is a living document, so you can add and subtract characteristics from it at any time.

When we talk about settling, you'll begin to understand how important this list is. Now, I know, even this deep into the book, some of you are thinking you don't need to commit your list to paper. You know your list. You've had it in your head forever. You know exactly what you're looking for.

I'm here to tell you that you need to write the list down to make it real.

Why do you have to make it real? Because some man is going to come along who's good-looking or has a great laugh. He'll compliment your macaroni and cheese. The stars in your eyes will inevitably make that list fly right out of your head, and you'll forget all about the fact that he doesn't meet any of the characteristics on your list, and, in the end, you'll have wasted all kinds of time and energy on a man because he complimented your macaroni and cheese.

In the dating game, the list gives you the markers and the reference points of the items you're looking for. The list keeps you focused.

So let's say you're looking through the haystack for your needle. You've got your list. You know exactly what you're looking for. You are sorting through that pile of hay, and maybe you're not finding that needle yet, but you're willing to keep looking.

Then, you find a needle. This needle is not as long as the needle you were looking for. It may not be as sharp as the one you're looking for. It fits some of the characteristics you have on your list because you've come up with a plethora of things you'd like your needle to have. But it doesn't fit all of them. Still, it's a pretty darn good needle. So, you settle for the one in the hand rather than tossing it back into that haystack and searching again.

Got it?

You haven't violated one of your standards. It's still a needle. It still pricks your finger; it still stitches things together.

THERE'S NOTHING REALLY WRONG WITH THE NEEDLE. IT'S JUST NOT THE EXACT ONE YOU HAD IN MIND WHEN YOU CREATED YOUR LIST.

Here's another example of settling that applies whether you're dating or not.

You're out with family and friends, and you're all hungry, so you go to a restaurant. You look at the menu and realize it's mostly seafood. Now, my family, especially my husband, loves seafood. I don't. Still, I'm hungry, so I will find something else on that menu that is not seafood. I will settle for that something else because I still need to satisfy my hunger.

I'm on a search for food. It's not exactly what I wanted. It doesn't fit everything on my list, but it's still going to feed me, and it won't kill me to compromise a bit.

Let's go back to that almost perfect man—or woman—you found. I'm going to stick with the perfect man for a bit here because, let's face it, most of the people who will feel the need to read a book like this will be women. Men need it too. They just won't admit it!

ACCORDING TO GWENDOLYN SEIDMAN PHD IN AN ARTICLE IN *PSYCHOLOGY TODAY* (FEB. 25, 2017), THE MOST IMPORTANT QUALITIES FOR A HAPPY RELATIONSHIP ARE:
1. KINDNESS, LOYALTY, AND UNDERSTANDING;
2. SIMILARITY;
3. CONSCIENTIOUSNESS;
4. EMOTIONAL STABILITY;
5. THE BELIEF THAT RELATIONSHIPS TAKE WORK.[20]

Anyway, you roll up on someone who has all the characteristics you want. He's good-looking, has a great laugh, is financially secure, and he complimented you on your macaroni and cheese. He is as close to perfect as you've encountered, but he's five feet tall. Now, some women will go find a stepladder and have a marriage to last a lifetime. A woman like that settled. She didn't lower her standards. She decided seven feet tall wasn't all it was cracked up to be.

Settling takes into consideration what you might receive if you make yourself open to characteristics that aren't game changers for you. He may not be this, but he is *that*. In the world surrounding your search for the needle, you need to understand what you can't live without—your standards—and what you might be willing to settle for. That's why I say you need to make your list a physical thing and understand which is which so you can make wise decisions.

To some, height may be a standard; for others, it may not. What is important is that you know the difference between the two *for you*. One of the most beautiful people could be in a package you pushed aside because you didn't like the wrapper.

Know your list and know the difference between settling and standards.

Here's another example. You come across a man or woman who you know has a history of physical abuse against their former partners. They have a great job, they look great, they might even be charming and funny. Would you go out with them anyway, thinking you could change them?

If you say yes to that, that's not settling. That's lowering your standards. I don't care if you're single and desperate and have been out there looking for years. Accepting a physically abusive relationship is lowering standards. No one deserves that no matter how alone a person feels or how tired of the search they are.

Now, don't get me wrong. People who have a history of physical abuse can get help, but they need to get professional help. Don't be fooled into thinking you can fix them. The same can be said for people who have had addiction problems, mental health issues, or have even done the time for their crimes. These people can be redeemed, reformed, and forgiven. That said, going into a relationship thinking you can fix anger issues, addiction problems, or other clinically treatable issues on your own is just stupid. Love may be able to heal some ills for a time, but it's only temporary. It may help to serve as motivation for them to finally tackle their issues, but it is not on you to convince them of this.

List your standards and list all the things you could consider settling for because God could be sending you someone right now! It could be someone who may not look the part, but they could have all the pieces you've been missing that will lead to a successful relationship.

I love sweets. Cake, pies, or a candy bar ... you name it. The pie may not be here, but I'll settle for a cookie. I'll eat that cookie, and my sweet tooth will still be satisfied. I won't change my standard and have potato chips instead.

Which brings me back to that list. You need to put your list on paper and keep it focused in your mind. It's not just a list of things you want in a partner. You know it well enough to understand what things you can live without and compromise on and what things are game changers. This is no one else's search. This is yours.

Now, pay attention here. Sometimes, it takes a level of maturity to understand the difference between standards and settling. Young people tend to get confused between the two and then choose wrong because they don't understand compromise. They think settling is a bad thing.

Say you're a young man who likes a thick woman. You meet a lady who is beautiful, intelligent, kind, has all the attributes you've been looking for ... everything you want in a woman. Only problem is, she is skinny. She looks like she needs a sandwich! The young man says, "I ain't going for that. She's too skinny." He's so focused on the wrapper, he doesn't take the time to look inside the box. That's a demonstration of his immaturity.

Now, if you're older, and the standards on your list are still all based on the exterior, I'm going to be honest with you right here. You're not ready to date. You need to walk away and finish playing. This book is for the mature.

At some point in time, you can come back to this book when you're ready to compromise on appearance and some of those surface things that mean little. When you realize appearance is not going to kill you and you determine what is important to you, you may be mature enough to understand the difference between settling and standards.

In the next chapter, we'll clarify a few more points to consider when compiling your list and then do some fine-tuning.

CHAPTER SEVEN
The Red Flag
(or the Compromise)

red-flag ('red-'flag), red-flagged; red-flagging; red-flags,
transitive verb, to identify or draw attention to
(a problem or issue to be dealt with)

red flag, *noun,* a warning signal or sign[21]

W hen I started praying for help to find a husband, I had my list of things I wanted to find in a future partner, just like the list I've told you to write. And, like yours, my list wasn't written in cement. The list is a living document. It is meant for you to change and update or refine as you go along and it helps you focus on finding the characteristics you seek when you meet someone new. In addition to your list of what you want, you may find it helpful to create a list of what you don't want. Here's what I mean.

I had a list, but it still took me years to find my husband. In the meantime, there were stumbles. Despite knowing my list very well and being very sure of what it was I wanted, when people with characteristics that were *not* on my list found me, I found myself doing what so many of us do: I compromised.

So why do we compromise? Maybe it's because someone you know and love tells you that a particular man would be good for you. Despite knowing this person has things on your Do Not Compromise list, your mother is telling you to reconsider. How can you turn her down? Your instincts may be ringing like an emergency alarm that this man isn't right for you, but you love and respect your mother and don't want to go against her wishes or hurt her feelings. So, you compromise.

Maybe you've been through a rough patch and have just run into someone you knew from back in the day. You're looking for comfort, for familiarity. This man you knew back when life was simpler wasn't good for you then. He's probably not good for you now, but that familiar pull gives you the security you need at the time, so you compromise.

IN HER ARTICLE, "11 RED FLAGS IN A RELATIONSHIP NOT TO IGNORE," ROSSANA SNEE, A LICENSED MARRIAGE AND FAMILY THERAPIST, SAYS, IT'S EASIER TO SPOT PROBLEMS IN SOMEONE ELSE'S RELATIONSHIP THAN IT IS YOUR OWN. "IF IGNORED, RED FLAGS IN A RELATIONSHIP CAN TURN AN APPARENTLY ROMANTIC RELATIONSHIP INTO AN UGLY AND PAINFUL ALLIANCE."[22]

Sometimes, it doesn't matter how well someone knows you; they don't always know what it is you need. Even if you grew up together, they may have no idea what experiences you've had in the past that brought you to this point in your life, nor will they know what's on your list. Friends and family can be great matchmakers for you (we will talk about that in a later chapter), but not always. Before you get lost in all these distractions, you're going to need to refer to your list.

Distractions are one reason why the list is so important. You will use that list so you can always focus on what you are searching for. That way those essential things aren't lost to you in the heat of some emotional moment, whether that involves pleasing someone else or comforting an immediate hurt. The list helps you stay sure-footed in your quest.

When you're making your list, be specific.

Maybe you could start your list with the qualities you found attractive in other people even though things didn't work out. When you're making your list, it's important to consider what you tried before, the boxes you thought you could check off that didn't bring you the result you expected.

For example, maybe one of the characteristics you've been looking for is a man who is soft-spoken. So you went and found yourself a soft-spoken man, only to discover that he had a horrible temper that manifested itself in dangerous ways. Still, you may want to keep that soft-spoken nature on your list.

Now, here's where we talk about your new list. This second list is your red-flag list.

The red-flag list is unlike your desires list because it's more of a reference point. If a man has one of the characteristics on your red-flag list, it doesn't automatically mean they are disqualified.

> "I LOVES HARPO. GOD KNOWS I DO. BUT I'D
> KILL HIM DEAD BEFORE I LET HIM BEAT ME."
> —SOFIA IN *THE COLOR PURPLE*[23]

For example, remember that soft-spoken man you found before. He had a temper that manifested itself dangerously, so you put "dangerous temper" on your red-flag list. A man with a temper isn't necessarily dangerous. We all can lose our temper now and then. But how a man reacts to things that make him mad could be a red flag. What exactly ignites his anger? Is his temper slow to boil or instant? Are there things you do naturally that make him lose his temper?

The most important thing to ask yourself about this man's temper is, can you tolerate it? If "even-tempered" is on your list, is that something you think you could compromise on or something you could settle for?

The red-flag list is my reference point for what didn't work for me in the past. It's a reminder that I've tried this already. I've already discovered I have zero tolerance for a man who will lose his temper when I spend time with my girlfriends, for example. That's a red flag. I've been there before. I know it won't work. Losing his temper at me for having personal time is on my Do Not Compromise list.

Now, does he lose his temper for some other things? His temper will go on my red-flag list if there are certain things about his anger that I will not tolerate. If, however, his loss of temper this time is over something that seems reasonable, it shouldn't raise a red flag for you.

As mentioned, the red-flag list should be used as a reference point. It's not about being judgmental. There is no judgment here. We all have our own lines in the sand. Our tolerance levels are going to be different.

While still searching for my husband, I remember asking God for a dark-skinned man. Then, long before I met my husband, God put before me what I asked for: a dark-skinned man. Exactly what I prayed for, right?

But even though he had one of the characteristics I'd prayed for, his character did not measure up. He was what I would call "a player." I simply couldn't have that. The overall package wasn't right for me.

After that one encounter with a dark-skinned man and the hurt—well, not hurt, exactly … he didn't really hurt me …. Perhaps the *disappointment* I felt in that encounter made me size up and consider every man I met who fit that failed item on my list. I had it in my head, perhaps in my subconscious, that dark-skinned men were players. Again, don't judge me. I was learning and growing, and, let's be honest—you've done it too. We sometimes assign characteristics to people or make generalizations about them based on our history with someone else. Maybe you had a bad experience with a professional athlete or someone who works in a particular field, and everyone else you meet who does that for a living gets slotted into that same negative space. It happens.

It's like that Usher song, "U Remind Me," where he laments that every time he looks at his current love interest, he is reminded of someone else who put him through something terrible. It's this constant reminder that makes him realize the new relationship will never work.

He's saying, "We can't be together because you remind me of someone who broke my heart."

Yes, it happens, but it's not always an accurate measurement. As I said in my best-selling self-help book, *The Death of the Angry Black Woman*, your subconscious can be a dangerous thing. It's a powerful thing. You have a negative reaction or find something you cannot tolerate in someone, and that red flag remains in your subconscious. Then you start a new search, and you find yourself realizing, this is the same individual in style, color, personality, class, whatever it is, who didn't work out before.

This is why I began doing the opposite. This is why I began doing the opposite. In this case, the dark-skinned man had not worked out. I started dating light-skinned guys.

Guess what? They didn't work out either!

THE TRUTH IS, YOU CAN'T RUN FROM YOU. YOU CAN CHANGE
PARTNERS, BUT YOU'LL STILL BE DANCING ALONE.

The item on my list of desired things was a dark-skinned man. But the dark-skinned man I met was a player. That shouldn't have meant I needed to take dark-skinned men off my list. It meant I needed to put players on my red-flag list!

What if you've dated an athlete who spent a great deal of time preening in front of mirrors or looking for admiration, and you couldn't stand that? That doesn't mean you should take athletes off your list. It means you should put extreme vanity on your red-flag list.

What I desired and what I most wanted in a relationship changed over the years. My life experiences and the people I encountered all influenced what I most desired in personality, in appearance, in ethnicity, and in class. My wants changed and grew as I grew, and

I understood more of myself as I gathered data and searched the heap. I built the perfect person in my subconscious, and I went on a quest to find my match.

Eventually, I understood the things I needed for me. I understood the kind of man I desired most.

It took some work to find and identify the things I really wanted. This is exactly why developing your list of desired qualities should be a living document. You need to be willing to put things on and take them off as you grow and as the discovery of yourself changes. Just as your list of desires grows, your red-flag list will grow—or shorten. You may learn there are some things you are more capable of tolerating as you journey on your quest.

When it was time for me to find my fit—because that's what I call my husband, my perfect fit—he had a bit of all the qualities I had searched for on my quest in one person. Instead of avoiding him because of his dark skin, I focused on his qualities, his character, his personality. It was easy to identify him when I found him. I was able to recognize in him all the things I had studied during my dating, during my own growth.

REMEMBER THE COMPANY WHERE YOU BUILD YOUR OWN BEAR? YOU CAN GO INTO THE STORE AND CHOOSE THE EYES, STUFFING, CLOTHES, AND SHOES. YOU PUT IT ALL TOGETHER, AND IT RUNS THROUGH THE MACHINE AND—LIKE FINDING YOUR FIT—OUT COMES YOUR PERFECT, CUSTOM-BUILT BEAR.

The search is long and can be very hard, but remember, you are learning and growing in this experience, and that growth will help you build your bear.

When you've developed your list with all the characteristics and personality traits you most desire, you may want to pray on it. "God, he's handsome," "she's beautiful, she's loving," "he's kind, he's meek," "she's compassionate," "he likes food, he doesn't like food," "she's witty," or "he's serious and intelligent … ." All these things could be on your list and could be part of your prayers. These traits only make it onto your list because you've gathered the data you need to understand what you can tolerate, what you need, and what makes up the list of things you most want and drives your quest.

Remember, dating is gathering data. You don't come to the date saying you want this man. You don't come saying you want this woman.

You come to the date saying to yourself that you are gathering the data you need to determine if this person meets the qualities with which you believe you can build something lasting ... and vice versa. It's gotta work both ways. Never invest in one person too fast. You've got to gather your data to determine, even if the date went well, whether or not your quest should continue.

And one final thought: It helps to have people assisting in your quest. Remember when we talked about friends and family suggesting someone to you? Well, they may not be the best judge of who is right for you, but they may help you stay focused on what is on your desired list and on your red-flag list. When you have the right people looking out for you, they may be able to help you see and acknowledge things you might not have seen on your own.

FINE-TUNING YOUR LIST

Take another look at the list of characteristics you'd like to find in your needle. With the previous chapter in mind, on what things would you be willing to compromise? On what things would you be willing to settle? What things are on your red-flag list?

Compromise	No Compromise (Red-Flag list)
Examples: I might be willing to travel for a long-distance relationship.	I will not date someone who smokes.

CHAPTER EIGHT
Slim Pickings

I am writing this a few days before Christmas, and I must confess: My Thanksgiving turkey is still on my mind. I've been thinking about it for weeks because I have to admit, however grudgingly, that my Thanksgiving turkey this year did not look the best. It was not a pretty bird. We put a lot of seasoning on it and injected it with a lot of butter, and I'll be honest with you—it was very dark, a lot darker than a turkey ought to be. I stared at that bird and did not have high hopes.

Then my husband took a knife, and he sliced into that bird. And, *oh my!* I'm telling you, that meat inside was succulent, juicy, moist, and fresh. There was nothing burnt, nothing dried out about that meat. The outside wasn't burnt either. It was just that the seasoning had it looking a deeper brown, almost black, and I hadn't expected that.

Though people might have been talking about my bird and giving me a hard time when they saw it, when they tasted it, they had to shut up. That turkey was amazing.

I love Thanksgiving turkey, but I think I love the turkey leftovers almost as much. The leftovers from the bird this year were equally as juicy and delicious as they were on day one. We attacked that carcass until we'd stripped the breast meat, the wing meat, and everything on the thighs and legs. When we began to pick through the back meat, we knew we were nearing the end. We were still working at getting every piece of meat we could off those bones because even though it hadn't looked very good when it came out of the oven, every bite, every sliver had the potential to make a perfect turkey sandwich. Eventually, no matter how hard we looked and picked at it, we couldn't find any more meat.

ACCORDING TO A 2019 U.S. CENSUS BUREAU REPORT, THE PERCENTAGE OF PEOPLE WHO NEVER MARRY IS ON THE RISE. WHEN RACE IS FACTORED IN, THE DIFFERENCES ARE SUBSTANTIAL. IN FOR THOSE AGE FIFTY-FIVE AND OVER, THE PERCENTAGE OF WHITE WOMEN (NON-HISPANIC) WHO HAVE NEVER MARRIED IS 6 PERCENT. FOR BLACK WOMEN IN THE SAME AGE CATEGORY, THE RATE IS 17 PERCENT.[24]

When I think about that turkey, I think about how we go through life, searching so hard for that one good piece of meat. We're living our lives through work and play, trying to find one good person, that perfect fit in the midst of all that we deal with from day to day. We need just one good person who will stand the test of time.

Now, I'm sure you've heard the expression that there are slim pickings out there. We hear it all the time in magazines, in the news, on talk shows, and when we're talking among ourselves. The statistics don't lie.

The biblical reference is, "And seven women shall take hold of one man in that day, saying, 'We will eat our own bread and wear our own clothes, only let us be called by your name; take away our reproach'" (Isaiah 4:1, ESV).[25]

Years ago, the ratio of women to men in the United States was terrible, as bad as eleven women to one man in some cities. The demographics have shifted a bit, but statistically, there are still more women in America than men. Nationally, the ratio is much closer to one to one. The ratio grows even more uneven as we get older because women still tend to outlive men. Now, in all but a few states, women still outnumber men, but the ratios vary from state to state and city to city.

I know I'm not telling you anything new when I point out that the numbers in the African American community are different. While the ratios are close to one to one (52 percent women and 48 percent men according to the same census report from 2019[26]), there are plenty of other factors—such as education barriers, incarceration, and other issues of systemic racism—that make finding the needle in a haystack in our community a far more statistically difficult thing to do. According to an article published in *The Washington Post*,[27] Diane M. Stewart writes, "The majority of black women in America are single by circumstance, not by choice, and the statistics are jarring."

THE 2018 US CENSUS REVEALED, FOR EXAMPLE, THAT IN 2009, 71 PERCENT OF BLACK WOMEN IN AMERICA ARE UNMARRIED.[28]

Let me repeat: 71 percent of black women in America are single and not by choice. So let's be honest. Slim pickings!

I need you to hear me when I say that horrible statistic is not everyone's story. After all, there are at least 29 percent of us who are married. But let's be honest again. This book is called *A Needle in a Haystack* for a reason. And we've been talking about impossible searches for a reason. If we're going to talk about statistics, know that 29 percent may not seem like a lot, but what it does signify is that it is not impossible. It *is* possible.

Suppose I told you there *is* somebody for you. The 29 percent proves there *is* a possibility and that this *is* obtainable. Sometimes, some of us have work to do on ourselves. We talked about that in *The Death of the Angry Black Woman.* We have to do some work on ourselves, and I'm not talking just about anger issues or even appearance issues. This is hard work. It takes time. It will also take stamina and determination, but just know that it is obtainable.

I'm here to tell you, yes, there are slim pickings out there, but finding your fit is obtainable with time, work, and a little bit of prayer. I'm telling you this because I did that. I believe—and I'm using the word "believe" for a reason—that if it happened for me, it can happen for you, too, if you want it to.

As African American women and men, we have to accept that many of us who might have been part of our haystack are caught up in the legal system. Whether you agree with it or not, a portion of our potential haystacks will be seeking same-sex relationships. And whether you agree with it or not, a portion of our haystacks will be people who prefer to seek a relationship with someone outside of their race. Those are the facts.

I don't know what your particular story is, but I'm going to ask you not to be overwhelmed by these statistics or by the ways your potential pickings are reduced. Release any frustration or anger you may feel about those realities and move on. I'm going to ask you to turn the page on that and stay with me.

Your list is good for a lot of reasons, one of which is, it helps you broaden your mind and notice things you might have missed when you created your list in the first place. Knowing these statistics, understanding the realities, accepting the truth about slim pickings, and knowing the difference between settling and your red flags— what would you think if the person who found you was of a different race?

What if I told you the silver needle you are searching for in that haystack is a golden needle or wooden or even made of glass? All those needles do their job, don't they? During your search through the heap, as you're digging through the rubble, you have no idea what kind of needle you will find. Your position is to prepare to find the needle that will best fit the job you need it for.

This is why we're here.

Sometimes, as you are searching, you might find a needle that is cheap, broken, or rusted and bent. If you don't know your own worth, you might be able to convince yourself that this is the kind of needle you deserve.

Let me repeat.

WHEN WE DON'T KNOW OUR OWN WORTH, WE MAY CONVINCE OURSELVES THAT WE FIND THE LOVE WE DESERVE. YOU ARE WRONG!

If you're digging through that haystack, and all you can come up with are cheap, broken, rusted, or bent needles, instead of accepting them as if you deserve defective needles, maybe you need to search some other haystack. Don't be limited by the heap you are searching in. Try a different heap.

Here it is more plainly: love comes in all types of shapes and sizes and colors. Your list is based off an idea you have in your head, and that's fine. I told you to write your list. I'm going to guess that you wrote down the appearance and characteristics you have always used when searching for your fit. But the list is a living document, so I want to give you an opportunity to revisit it now and consider ways you might broaden that list.

I have a sister who has been happily married for years. Her husband happens to be a white man. Am I telling you to date outside your race? No. I'm not advocating for or against anything. I'm merely saying that love comes in all kinds of shapes and sizes and colors. I'm advocating for love. You can fill in those blanks any way you choose.

Pickings are slim! Sometimes, we may need to face reality and say, "Pickings may be slim in my community." "Pickings may be slim in my church." "Pickings may be slim in the places where I hang out." Pickings *are* slim! They are. So you need to get a bit more creative. Open your mind and heart.

My sisters and brothers, you have got to do something different. If you are reading this book, you already know that. Again, I'm not saying your match is someone of another race. I'm simply saying, if you keep turning to your type, and it's not working, you need to be open to changing your type. You need to be willing to revisit your list.

Let me tell you something else. Sometimes, we have an idea of an individual we want to pick, but God has his own idea of the one he wants to choose for us. You get stuck because you're still picking in that same old haystack, in the same old place you've always searched.

Man, we picked the hell out of that turkey. We kept going back to that bird because we had already tasted that something special was there for us. That certainty lured us back to that bird for the taste and the smell over and over again.

At some point, you will be lured to a place where you can be found, but you have to be open to it. You have to open your senses in your search and broaden your mindset.

One Sunday, God taught me that sometimes people can't see the sea because their spirit has been programmed to see lakes. Sometimes, you can program your body and mind to focus on a community instead of opening your mind to the world. There is a sea of people out there. But if you refuse to see them and confine yourself to the slim pickings of your community, you make your search much more difficult.

Remember what I said earlier about insanity? It's doing the same thing over and over again and expecting a different result. If the same thing isn't working, you need to try something different. Get a passport and take a trip. Join a travel club. Explore new hobbies. Do something you've always wanted to do but didn't.

Slim pickings are slim because you won't go out on a limb to extend your search.

My family gave me such a hard time on social media about my bird. They bashed it, but they can't deny that they mined those slim pickings until there was nothing left. That turkey was huge when we started on it, and we ate it until our bellies were full and kept eating it until there was nothing left.

Some of you are starving in your dating search. But you've picked at that carcass until there's nothing left. You already know the people in your community. You already know the people in your church. You've spent months searching through the preferences you set up on dating sites, and you've had all the blind dates your friends have suggested. And you can try new places to search, but if you're still looking for the same type, if you haven't made any adjustments to your list, do you think the results in a new place might be the same?

One final thought about slim pickings. Eventually, after all that picking, we had to throw that carcass away because it was done. There was nothing left to eat. But we don't have to throw away anything on your list. I just ask you to approach it with an open mind and understand that we don't know what will come looking for us. We simply have to be ready to be found when it comes.

So this is what we're going to do. I've asked you to write your lists—the good things and the bad. Now, I ask you to consider these lists as the outline of the person you really want. The outline will include the things you will consider now that your horizons are broader, and your mind is more open to possibilities. Once we draw that outline, you can color it in with your own box of crayons.

YOUR BOX OF CRAYONS

It's time to revisit your list again. After reading the previous chapter, are there more things on your list you can adjust to **expand your haystack?** In what ways can you ensure that perfectly good needles aren't dismissed without consideration?

Examples:
- I will consider dating someone who is younger/older than me by five to ten years.
- Race and ethnicity will not be factors in my needle search.

CHAPTER NINE
Put That Back!

budget (ˈbə-jət), *transitive verb,* to put or allow for in a
statement or plan coordinating resources and expenditures: to put
or allow for in a budget; to require to adhere to a budget; to allocate
funds for in a budget; to plan or provide for the use of in detail[29]

When I was a kid, we'd get excited on Saturdays because we knew that was the day Mommy would take us to Key Foods in Brooklyn for grocery shopping. Living on a budget, as we all do, my mother would make a list of things she intended to buy, and she stuck to it. Once she had her list done, there wasn't a lot of wiggle room.

Before we even walked in the door, she would say three words. I'm sure these are the same three words every black woman has said to a child before entering any kind of store. She'd look at us, put a serious expression on her face, and say in a way that meant you best pay attention, "Don't touch nothin'!"

The majority of the time, I would heed that warning. But one day, as we entered the cereal aisle, I immediately spotted a new cereal based on the cartoon character Strawberry Shortcake—a little, puffy-cheeked, redheaded kid wearing a pink, fluffy bonnet and dress, and she had a cat named Custard. On the cereal box, she held a pint of strawberries and she poured a pitcher of milk onto a bowl overflowing with pink, crunchy-looking cereal.

Now, you should know that I have always been partial to strawberry shortcake—the dessert, not so much the cartoon. I am a big fan, so when I saw that cereal, it spoke to me. I'd heard my mother's instructions, but this was *strawberry shortcake* in a *cereal*. How could I possibly pass that up?

I noticed my mother's back was turned, but you know how mothers are. They have eyes in the backs of their heads. As soon as I took that cereal off the shelf and put it in the cart, she scolded, "Put that back."

It startled me, but not enough to diminish my desire to taste that cereal. I just wanted to take it home, to keep the box with all the strawberries and this cute, redheaded kid and her cat. But the authority in my mother's voice told me she wouldn't broker any nonsense. So, I did what kids usually do in this situation. I begged.

"Please, Mommy. You know I love Strawberry Shortcake, and I love Custard the cat, and, and, and ...."

Begging didn't usually work with my mother, but that time it did! She bent her rules and let me have the cereal. She took the Cheerios out of the cart and put them back on the shelf, making the exchange so that I could have what I thought I really wanted, and she could still stay on her budget.

But when she first told me to put it back, being a child, I couldn't understand what her objection might be. I didn't understand why she would deny me this thing I wanted so much, or that buying it might not have been in her budget. I didn't understand that the cereal might be filled with sugar and not good for me. All I knew was she was preventing me from having what I really and truly wanted.

What do I want you to get out of this story?

It's simple. Sometimes we want something because of what it looks like or how appealing it is on the outside, even though what's inside may not be suitable for us.

IT'S LIKE FLIES OR MOTHS TO A FLAME. WE LOVE GOOD-LOOKING
PEOPLE. WE FLUTTER ABOUT THEM AND CAN'T SEEM TO PULL
OURSELVES AWAY, WHETHER THEY ARE GOOD FOR US OR NOT.

As you look over the list you've been working on, I'm going to guess you'll see some things on there that you don't really need, but you want them anyway. Like me as a child, you're drawn to the packaging more than the product inside. We somehow care about hair color, eye color, skin color, and shade. We care about height, dress size, breast size, even shoe size.

Sometimes, it pays to give yourself a few instructions before you venture into the dating store, instructions like the one my mother gave. She said, "Put that back." What she was really saying is, we need to resist the inclination to grab things that look a certain way but aren't in our budget.

In this case, I'm not talking about budget in terms of money but in value. I'm talking about your worth. I'm talking about how you need to understand your own value and assess your worth. What if I told you there are some things you need to put back because either that thing doesn't appreciate your true value, or its lack of value will diminish yours?

You need to handle your finances. In dating, that means sizing up the individuals you come in contact with. And when you do this, you can't have your clock ticking in the background. Time is fleeting, and many of you set deadlines for yourselves, but when it comes to your relationship budget, time shouldn't be a factor. Take the time to understand this because it is worth the investment.

I was distracted by the very thought of strawberries. The idea that I could have my favorite dessert in a breakfast cereal, well, that was just a perfect combination in my young eyes. We often get distracted by the lights and the flags and the beauty of the things we see. We get excited. We think that burst of feeling we have when we've shared a look with someone means something deeper than it does. The hello with a smile hits us in the pit of our stomach, and we think that means something special. The siren call of beauty can often drown out our conscious thoughts—that one telling us to "put that back."

Your conscious is telling you that the thing you've picked up doesn't fit where you want it to go.

> YOUR HEAD IS TRYING TO TELL YOU THERE IS A
> PROBLEM WITH SUITABILITY HERE, BUT YOU'RE NOT LISTENING.
> IF YOU TOOK A MOMENT TO BREATHE, YOU'D REALIZE
> YOU'RE SO CAUGHT UP WITH THE EXTERIOR, YOU HAVE
> NO IDEA WHAT'S HAPPENING ON IN THE INSIDE. SUCH TIMES ARE
> WHEN YOU TRULY NEED TO LISTEN AND PUT THAT BACK.

I took that cereal home, poured a great big bowl of it, and covered it in milk. It did not taste like strawberry shortcake. My mother had been right. I should have put that back. I got a pair of scissors and cut Strawberry Shortcake and Custard the cat out from the box and stuck them on my wall. I never finished the cereal.

Here are some of the mistakes we make with grabbing things off the shelves when we know we should have put them back. I bet you will recognize some of these common "impulse buys" if you haven't already.

Some of us get involved with an ex. *Again.* And you know you should have put that back. Maybe you got tired of your search for the right fit. Maybe you got frustrated. Maybe there are other stressors in your life that made you crave some comfort, something familiar, but in the end just left you feeling empty. You really should have put that back.

If it's not the ex, it's someone of the same type as your ex. You gravitate toward someone of the same height, shape, or profession. The same skin shade, haircut, or way of dressing with little regard for what is going on inside that person. In fact, there's nothing on the inside that can fill us up. You should have put that one back.

Or maybe you're just attracted to the shiny, beautiful thing that came your way. You think you're lucky because shiny and beautiful is paying attention to you, but you've had no chance to find out what is really going on with that person. And like me begging Mommy for that box of cereal as if it were the one thing I really, truly wanted, you've been blinded by the shine. Even your friends are telling you to put it back, but you are so excited by this shiny thing that you override their voices. You tell them they don't understand.

Beautiful does not mean bad or empty. People who are beautiful need love too! You simply need to bring a level of maturity to your search so that you aren't blinded by the shine. You need to be ready to acknowledge that sometimes, you can't hang onto that beauty when the shine starts to fade because you're coming to a better understanding of what's on your inside. You need to know when your budget, your standards, and your list cannot afford the expenditure of your emotions. You need to learn to choose what's good for you and which people are going to be good to you.

We've talked about settling and your red-flag list. The red-flag list comprises all the things on which you will never compromise. But in settling, this person could have some real redeeming qualities. What if that Strawberry Shortcake cereal had some amazing nutritional value in it? I didn't stop long enough to read the label; I just snatched it off the shelf. When I ate it, I was disappointed with the taste, but what if I hadn't realized that it actually was very good for me?

Now, consider this: a person might have characteristics on which you might have settled if you had given those characteristics the time to emerge. Instead, you jumped in with both feet; you pulled them off the shelf too quickly. Before you actually knew what you were getting into, they assigned their own set of values to your actions. They have determined that your immediate acceptance means you're not as serious about finding a true fit as they are. How could you be? In their eyes, you're just out for immediate gratification since you haven't taken the time to truly get to know who they are.

If you met someone who has amazing characteristics in your needs category—loves to laugh, deep sense of honesty, strong sense of family, stable and steady, for example—you should realize that these aren't things you're going to learn quickly. It takes time to understand someone's true character. To make it more difficult, if the packaging doesn't match what you have in your wants category, and you're not willing to give them the time you'd need to learn these things about them, whose loss will this be?

It is a natural thing to be attracted to shiny things; that's why they call it *attraction*. Your eyes are drawn to it. When you see beautiful art, your soul is filled with it. When we hear beautiful music and it swells and fills a room, it can bring tears to our eyes.

Beauty stirs emotion. Be careful and don't be fooled by it.

My mother allowed me to have what I wanted. She put the Cheerios back so that I could have my wish, even though what I wanted was basically dyed, crunchy sugar. It wasn't good for me. But I wanted what I wanted.

I know some of you are reading this and thinking about a past relationship when you should have put that sucker back on the shelf! Or you're thinking about the time you grabbed something from the shelf, but they put *you* back; if you'd taken the time to explore a bit longer, you might have learned their true worth. We make mistakes. Let's learn from them.

EXAMINE YOUR HISTORY

Think about your dating history. As discussed in the previous chapter, you should consider which relationships you should have put back on the shelf. More importantly, think about why you pulled them off the shelf in the first place.

Off the Shelf	Put Back on the Shelf
Example: Good-looking and made me laugh	Selfish and didn't consider my needs

CHAPTER TEN
Decorating with Style

I'm not bragging when I say that I have a knack for style and design. I love to make a statement with the way I dress, and I love to decorate.

One day, my husband and I decided to redecorate our office at church. He's not much of a decorator; he's more of a builder. So he relied on me to make the decorating decisions, which was smart on his part. Together with my sister, we made a trip to the store. He watched as I started pulling things off the shelves and loading up the cart.

"Babe, you're just tossing in all kinds of colors," he said. "Where are you going with this?"

My response to him was, "ROY G BIV."

"What is that supposed to mean?" he asked.

I repeated, "ROY G BIV."

He turned to my sister for a more understandable response.

She said, "Red, orange, yellow, green, blue, indigo, and violet. The colors in the rainbow. ROY G BIV."

It's a trick designers use to make you visualize all the colors in the rainbow in one stroke. The colors are listed in order of the length of the wavelength created by sunlight refracted in the raindrops in the sky, which create color and make up the rainbow. The longest wavelength is first (red), to the shortest (violet).

In decorating, you need to understand what happens when you mix colors together. If you blend the right ones, you end up with a pleasing third color. Examples: Red and yellow make orange. Yellow and blue make green. The same happens when you group colors together in accessories, rugs, art, and the like. Mix them properly, and you make beauty out of the chaos.

My husband, after hearing the explanation, was still doubtful.

"This isn't going to look good," he said.

I convinced him to have faith while we made the purchases and went back to the office. I asked him to just put the rug down, hang the things on the walls, and put the accessories around where I instructed.

At the end, we stepped back, and he was shocked.

"Wow," he said. "You've created something that I could not see."

I said, "ROY G BIV, baby. It's called blending."

What if I told you that the needle you will find in the haystack comes with a blended family? You're doing the looking, but truth be told, your needle is right now on the search for you as well. So this time, God has decided that your needle comes with five children. *Five* of them.

Is your response going to be, "I don't want someone else's children," "I don't want small children," or "I don't want someone who has children at all"?

First, you should know that each of these choices will make your haystack much smaller and more and more difficult to search. In fact, it may become so difficult to search that you may have taken yourself out of the equation altogether, depending on your age.

I'm forty-nine. My husband and I collectively have eight children. If "no children" had been on my standards list, if I had eliminated my husband from contention simply because he had had a full life before he met me, I would not be in the loving marriage I'm in now.

Still, I hear this often. You don't want anyone with children or young children or more than two children or [name your disqualifying thing about children].

I find it fascinating that people who desire to be found often have a plethora of things on their red-flag list that might not need to be there. Sometimes that red-flag list is longer than it truly needs to be. Often, people don't understand what love can do when mixed with the things one refuses to consider. How quickly would your list change if you were found by someone of a different race? How important would your standard of no children be to you if you were found by someone with a ready-made family?

You might tell God what you want, but that doesn't mean he's going to listen. Oftentimes, that's because we don't know what is available to us. We don't know what's there. Until we take the time to stand back and look, we don't see it.

God created ROY G BIV. He put all those colors together, and he knows what beauty they can make when they are blended together.

PEOPLE ARE JUDGMENTAL, BUT GOD IS LOVE,
AND LOVE IS COLOR-BLIND.

Imagine you're a single, African American woman with no children. Now, imagine God has sent you a man who is recently divorced, but he's rebuilding a life and is well on the way to recovering from the loss of his marriage. Now, imagine he has five children.

Could you be part of this blended family?

Now, imagine you're a single, African American man, and God sent you a woman who might be fighting cancer. Could you be there to love her while she's in the battle of her life?

God could send you someone who is unable to walk. He could send you the perfect match, but he is blind.

Sometimes it takes a special heart to see past some challenges to find your fit. ROY G BIV is representative of the beauty that can come from mixing things together that don't at first appear to fit at all. Our human eye will see things as being wrong until things are blended expertly and fit perfectly.

It takes a very strong person to see past black and white. It takes strength in character and heart to know that something is pushing you away, but you can move past that obstacle and get closer anyway.

I'm going to say this, and I bet most of you are going to agree. Have you ever turned the volume down in your car so that you could back up? You turn your music down so that you can see where you need to go. You know what I'm talking about.

NOISE SOMETIMES GETS IN THE WAY OF YOUR ABILITY TO SEE.

Love has a voice, and sometimes you need to remove the obstructions from your eyes to hear it. Let that love-voice speak to your heart. Every color in the rainbow can be mixed and blended to make something beautiful. It may be something you missed before. Listen closely and see it.

TURN DOWN THE NOISE

This chapter is about taking a deep breath, turning down the volume so you can see what you may have missed before. To get you started, here are a few questions to consider carefully. Take a long, hard look at relationship possibilities you've said no to in the past. Consider these questions:

- Are there dates you've turned down that you would **consider differently today?**
- Is there a first date that was a disaster, but if given the chance now, you would give that person **a second chance?**
- What about **missed opportunities?** Are there people you've met who you never asked out that you wish you had given another look?
- Now that you've tuned out the noise, **what would you change** if you had it to do all over again? What have you learned?

CHAPTER ELEVEN
Don't Touch This

approachable (ə′prō-ch ə-bəl), *adjective,* capable of being approached; accessible; specifically: easy to meet or deal with

similar: friendly, welcoming,
pleasant, agreeable, congenial, affable[30]

Some years ago, I took a class with Reverend Ronald B. Christian, pastor of Christian Love Baptist Church. He passed away in 2015, God rest his soul, but I was taking his class that happened to be scheduled directly after conference speaking engagements. When I arrived at the church, I was still dressed in my speaking attire, a look I had carefully put together because I knew I was going to appear before a large audience.

I wore a cranberry cream Escada suit. It was bad, and I knew it. It was well-tailored and looked professional and expensive, and the color was eye-catching. It was a perfect outfit, I thought, for grabbing my audience's attention and holding it during my presentation.

So after my presentation, I wore the outfit to Reverend Christian's class. I arrived a bit early and found the reverend relaxing before his presentation while grabbing a snack. When I said "hello," he said, "Girl, you look great."

"Thank you," I said and took my seat.

He started to teach the class, and about a minute into it, he turned to me, and he said, "Girl, you look great."

"Thank you," I said again. Of course, when he said that, all eyes turned to me. But I thanked him all the same, and he went on with teaching.

Not too long after that, he turned to me again, and he said, "Girl, you look great."

"Thank you," I said for the third time, beginning to get annoyed because I didn't understand what he was doing. He stopped and complimented me about five more times during his class. Was he being sarcastic? Was he just teasing me? I respected Reverend Christian enough to take his classes, and I always knew he had a method to his madness, but this time I was at a loss as to what he expected me to learn from this constant shift of not just his but the entire class's attention to me and my appearance.

He finally stopped and looked at me. "You see how I keep doing this? I'm doing this because you look so beautiful, you've become a distraction to the people you're trying to reach."

I froze. I started thinking to myself, if I'm going to a conference, shouldn't I try to look my best? I didn't understand what he expected of me.

"Is it better to look raggedy?" I asked him.

"No, but you do want to dress in a way that allows you to connect to the audience and for the audience to connect to you."

He went on to explain that my expensive suit and the beautiful color created a kind of interference with the connection I wanted to make. And while he thought I looked beautiful, I also looked unapproachable, which would make it difficult for the audience to hear the message I was trying to share with them.

"YOU WANT THEM TO REMEMBER YOUR WORDS," HE SAID, "NOT REMEMBER WHAT YOU WERE WEARING."

That was a *wow* moment for me.

Coming from anyone else, I may not have heard that message in the way it was delivered. But I respected Reverend Christian, and what he'd said made sense. However, I still had to wrestle with it a bit. Remember, I care about my appearance. I enjoy leaving an impression of *je ne sais quoi* with effortless style, a bold use of color, and confidence.

It took me a bit of time, but I came away with the lesson, and I'll never forget it.

Brothers, y'all look fabulous. Sisters, y'all look beautiful. There are days when you walk out the door, and there is no stopping you. You've got the hair and the clothes and the shoes and the nails and the makeup, and you are a bold, beautiful, living, breathing force that is amazing. I can sit back and admire y'all all day long. Our beauty is an awesome thing, and we know how to accentuate it and amplify it until it shines like a star. Am I right?

But there are many days when you look all put together, and that put-together look also says, "Don't touch this."

I was having a conversation with a young lady who wanted some relationship help. She wanted to know what she was doing wrong. This was a beautiful young woman who made sure her hair, makeup, and clothes were right every time she walked out the door. We're taught this, right? Always dress like you're going to run into your potential husband. Always look your best when you walk out the door.

But I suggested to her that she should try going out in a pair of jeans and sneakers for a change. "Wear a sweatshirt sometimes," I said.

She got angry. "Why should I dumb myself down?"

She wasn't ready to hear the lesson. I'm going to give the lesson to you.

There are times when we need to relax. When we are relaxed, we appear more approachable.

MAKEUP, HAIR, AND CLOTHES CAN BE LIKE A SHIELD
THAT WALLS YOU AWAY FROM THOSE WHO MAY APPRECIATE
WHAT THEY SEE BUT ARE EITHER INTIMIDATED BY THE
PERFECTION OR THINK THEY AREN'T WORTHY OF IT.

They may even look at you and wonder what is under all that perfection.

Here me now. There is nothing wrong with finding a way to relax.

The same reverend, Ronald B. Christian, who taught me about approachability, also taught me a lesson about transparency. One day, he said, "Go to work without makeup."

I thought, *Are you crazy? I'm a corporate girl.*

I knew I had some meetings and things the next day, but I wanted to be open to his lesson, so I wore far less makeup than I would have normally. I didn't go with a naked face, but I looked more natural than usual. It was a chance to allow my colleagues to see me without my corporate armor. If I could make myself vulnerable in that way in my workplace, do you think you might be willing to show that vulnerability to a potential love interest?

Now, don't get me wrong, and you may not want to hear this, but do not go out in a bonnet and a bathrobe. Bonnets and pajamas are not meant to be worn in the streets. Let me say it for the people in the back. Bonnets and pajamas are not meant to be worn in the streets! Slippers need to stay at home!

What I am saying is, know when to wear the lashes and when not to wear them. Make days when you're comfortable in a pair of sweats. Be willing to take off the armor and look more like your natural self.

You know, women like to see a hardworking man. We like it when they're a bit grimy and gritty. We tend to see that grit and grime as masculine, attractive, and a sign that he's a hard worker.

On the other hand, the expectation for women is to get dolled up. As women, we know there are varying levels of dolling up. The truth is, oftentimes, men are only being patient and understanding to our need to go through all those machinations. Sometimes, they try to see past all that.

When we go out on a date, we might think a particular level of personal preparation is necessary, but all the man is hoping for is that you will just be with him. He's already convinced you're beautiful. He doesn't need the layers of concealer and the lashes and three different lip colors. He just wants you to really *be* with him, without the wall of makeup perfection in the way. He wants you to be approachable.

To be approachable is to demonstrate a level of *realness*. You want them to get close enough to see that beyond the makeup and hair and general outward appearance, you really are cool, someone worth knowing. You may wear the eyelashes to emphasize and enhance the beauty of your eyes, but that beauty is still there when you take them off. Don't you want your man to know how your face looks when it's stripped of those accoutrements?

Remember what we talked about earlier when I told you to eat your wings and shut up? A lot happens between people without saying a word. We're all gathering data. A man may look at a woman he believes he can't afford based solely on her appearance. (Stop shaking your head. You know we all do it.) Would he find you more affordable if you weren't wearing your version of an Escada suit?

Take the suit off sometimes. Let me tell you, it works. It worked for me.

My husband and I had been virtually dating before we went to a conference together. When he saw me there for the first time in person and saw the way I dressed to give my ministry, he said, "If I would have met her [my conference persona] first, we wouldn't be here. When I met you first, you were just Jameliah. She was this cool chick who I could laugh with."

I'm so blessed he met the woman first and the persona later.

Sometimes, it's better for the man to meet the real woman first and the executive down the line.

Now, almost the opposite can be said of some men. Does your everyday look make it seem like you spend your life on the basketball court? Is your wardrobe filled with hoodies and Jordans? You need to demonstrate that you know how to dress for the occasion and not embarrass your potential fit by showing up to the wrong event dressed like you're the gardener. If you don't know what's expected, ask her! Don't assume the most casual look is the right one. It usually isn't.

Our desire to impress potential mates comes in all kinds of shapes and forms. We want to show them the business person up front. We want them to meet the Ivy League graduate, the independent person, the person who has their act together and their life straight. The real truth is, men and women want to know they can be of help, that they are needed.

Now you need to be careful, ladies. There are some men out there who see a woman who is put together and take advantage, if you know what I mean. We call them hobosapiens. Am I right? They will link themselves with you because they have nowhere to go. I've been there. I've been in that relationship. I'm out of it, and I won't go back. But you have to be careful because they can charm their way in when you least expect it. Women may pray for a lasting love, while some men prey on those women. Pray and prey have two very different meanings. It happens. Be aware.

But knowing there are predators can't keep you from searching for your fit. Relax. Go to the park. Leave your CHANEL shoes at home. Put on your jeans and sneakers.

We are all looking for a friend, someone who will be a comfort in the storm. Someone we can get close to. Your potential partner needs to see the approachable you. Can you put on jeans and sneakers and go on a long walk through a park? Are there sweatpants in your wardrobe so you can binge-watch a show together with a bowl of popcorn? When the corporate armor comes off, who is the real person inside? If the right wardrobe is important to you, then you know a suit isn't what one wears to dig through a haystack.

CHAPTER TWELVE
Time on My Side

Time is on my side, yes it is
Time is on my side, yes it is
Now you always say
That you want to be free
But you'll come running back (said you would baby)
You'll come running back (I said so many times before)
You'll come running back to me
—Lyrics by Jerry Ragovoy (aka Norman Meade)[31]

Even the most powerful people in the world cannot control time. During the pandemic of 2020, most of us learned that time really is not on our side.

We wish that we could put a time limit on our search for that perfect fit. We wish that we could extend the timetable for when we can have children. Having some sort of time limit might lower our frustration level, even help keep us from making stupid choices. We wish we could make a hard and fast deadline for the realization of all our aspirations. The truth of the matter is, we can't.

One of the greatest challenges of conducting your search for your needle in the haystack is that you need time to go through the pile of hay. You need time to make the right choices, to see what is suitable, to understand what is or isn't going to work for you. We need time to learn from our mistakes and to be able to recognize the counterfeit needles from the real ones.

One thing about time that we can all agree on is that it is frustrating. Since you can't control it, when time becomes a factor in your fortune or happiness, it can also become a barrier to achieving those things.

There's a Bible verse that talks about time. Even people who aren't familiar with the Bible will have probably heard this verse because it's so true, and we see it often in lyrics, poetry, and language. It says, "For everything there is a season, and a time for every matter under heaven: ... a time to love, and a time to hate; a time for war, and a time for peace" (Ecclesiastes 3:1, 3:8, ESV).[32]

I speak to women all over the world who ignore the fact that God has said there is a time for everything, literally everything under the heavens, but they insist on putting a time stamp on their wants and needs. They say, "By this date, I am going to be married. By this date, I'm going to have a child." Both women and men will do this.

I have often seen articles that list popular reasons—I tend to see them as excuses—men say they need to accomplish various things before they are ready for marriage. Many of the reasons given are predictable. They want a better career, more money, or to finish school. Then the excuses become a bit more elaborate. They want to buy a house or a better car. Okay, having a house and car are important, but are they really good reasons to delay marrying the woman you love?

One excuse I've seen often is the desire to have a passport. Seriously? Whether or not you have a passport is a reason to delay marriage? And often I've seen people say they want to use that passport to travel the world before they get married. Isn't travel something a couple can do together?

There are people who have taken the time to acquire all these things. They have a list of degrees, a successful career, a house, a car, and they've traveled the world.

Now what? They've checked off their list, and now they think their husband or wife is going to miraculously appear?

SOME PEOPLE TAKE THE TIME TO DO THE THINGS THEY THOUGHT WERE IMPORTANT, ONLY TO FIND THAT THE TIME THEY LOST WAS MORE IMPORTANT THAN THE THINGS THEY DID.

You ain't got the power to control time.

If you allow yourself to see what is put before you as you achieve your stated goals, time can be on your side.

What if you have a passport and travel the world but have your head and heart open for love while you do it? What if you sift through the haystack and search for your needle on an island somewhere? Or what if you end up sitting next to your needle on your flight?

Love has a job to do. Right now, as you read this, someone is searching for you. At some point, you need to put this book down and begin your search. I don't mean now! Keep reading. Make notes. Use a highlighter. I need you to finish this. But at some point, you need to walk away from whatever it is you're doing at the moment and see the world.

Time is something you cannot control.

Remember Strawberry Shortcake? I used to have a picture on my wall of her and Custard the cat. Strawberry is pictured walking along in her big, old, brown boots with Custard following. The caption on the picture reads, "Take some time along the way to see what's nice about today."

A 2017 SURVEY BY A BRITISH RESEARCHER FOR BRIDEBOOK.CO.UK SAYS COUPLES ARE WAITING MUCH LONGER TO MARRY. IN 1971, THE AVERAGE AGE WAS 22.6 YEARS FOR WOMEN AND 24.6 YEARS FOR MEN. IN 2017, THOSE AGES WERE 30.8 FOR WOMEN AND 32.7 FOR MEN. THE AVERAGE RELATIONSHIP LASTS 4.9 YEARS BEFORE MARRIAGE.[33] THE GOOD NEWS IS, ACCORDING TO THE OFFICE OF NATIONAL STATISTICS, DIVORCE IS ON A DOWNWARD TREND, FROM A PEAK OF 165,000 DIVORCES IN 1993 TO 108,000 IN 2019.[34]

It's a catchy rhyme but also a wise suggestion. It says to me that you can choose to use time in nicer ways, especially if you're feeling melancholy or frustrated about your search. Use some time to do something you put on the back burner or to discover new things about yourself.

Also, consider using some of the time to give your faith some work. Give it some substance. I've always said faith is an action word. Faith is what you do.

Operate your time instead of letting it slip through your fingers. Take time to work on you. See a therapist. Start a workout program. Work on you in a way that will make you proud of yourself and your accomplishments because pride in self shines through.

The real wasters of time are the things people do that are not beneficial to their growth. That is the biggest waste of time there is. You take something so precious and then waste it on regrets, revenge, or plain old thoughts of anger or negativity that suck the life out of you and drain you of time.

Time will flow whether you like it or not. The same goes for change. The Greek philosopher Heraclitus said, "Change is the only constant in life." It takes time to bring noticeable change. Time is the only thing given to us that we can use as we want. We would be fools if we didn't use it to make us better.[35]

In a couple of these chapters, we will talk about what I mean when I say "single and waiting." Here's a hint: If you're single and waiting—waiting for a career, for financial stability, for a house or a car—are you waiting and wasting time? Or are you using that time to make yourself better, to make yourself ready for the love that is searching for you now?

CHAPTER THIRTEEN
Matchmaking

My husband and I binge-watched the Netflix show by Shonda Rhymes, *Bridgerton*. Aside from thoroughly enjoying this sumptuous Regency romance, there were a few things to learn from the show in terms of dating.

Based on a series of romance novels by Julia Quinn, *Bridgerton* is set in Regency-era England—the early 1800s—when young women of wealthy families participated in a season's worth of events for the purposes of finding a husband. At a certain age, sometimes as young as sixteen, the young woman would "come out." Once out, these women had a matter of months to find a match. Those months would be filled with balls and fancy outings for the purposes of parading the young women around while people who supposedly knew what is best for them attempted to find an advantageous match.

If a young woman went the entire season and didn't find a suitable match, there was the fear that she might never be married and would instead become a spinster. I'll talk more about spinsters in a minute.

Even now, some communities, especially in the American South, still hold debutante balls. These days, such events are more about making political or career connections, but historically, debutante balls in early America were an extension of the British practice of putting the newly on-the-market young women on full display. The families of the debutantes would consider the prospect of a young man to decide how advantageous the match might be for both parties. Would the marriage improve their finances? Would making a current enemy part of the family settle some sort of long-standing dispute? Would the business prospects of both families benefit from a long-term partnership?

There are many cultures that believe in arranged marriages. Perhaps as early as birth, the parents have already decided who will marry and when. Some cultures use matchmakers. The matchmaker assesses the two families, the people who are ready for marriage, and then decides what the most advantageous match would be for everyone involved. The only way some matchmaker marriages can work is when both parties are open to the idea of learning to love the person who is chosen for them.

I'm sure most of you will be surprised to know that a matchmaker worked for me.

The man I married had been a long-time friend of my sister. My sister and I are close, but we have our own lives and separate circles of friends. My father is no longer with us, but my sister had introduced my now-husband to my father. I learned later that my father and my husband had many deep conversations that I knew nothing about. In fact, my sister and my husband were such close friends, he performed her marriage ceremony. I couldn't attend her wedding at the time, so I didn't meet him until years later. I know this all sounds complicated, and it was a little. Long story short, my sister knew my husband very well and knew me even better. She knew in her heart that my husband—her close friend and pastor—would be perfect for me. And she was right.

As I said, there are many cultures and religions that believe in arranged marriages. There are many parts of the Bible in which Jesus connected people together. Sometimes an arranged marriage is about what will come out of that union. Countries have achieved peace due to marriage. Have you seen the reality TV show *Married at First Sight* in which the first time the couple actually sees each other is on their wedding day?

The point is, for some people, there is something liberating about the idea of the people who know and understand you the best choosing someone who they think is best for you. Halle Berry once said that her picker was broken. Unlike some, Berry understood that she didn't know how to choose someone who was best for her.

WHO YOU SHOULD BE WITH AND POTENTIALLY MARRY MAY BE ONE OF THE MOST IMPORTANT DECISIONS OF YOUR LIFE, AND SOMETIMES, YOU NEED SOMEONE ELSE TO HELP MAKE THAT DECISION FOR YOU.

It may sound crazy, but it's not. A matchmaker can't just be anyone. A true matchmaker, who may come in the form of a very close friend or relative, will know your likes and dislikes and your strengths and weaknesses as well as all of that for the other person. They have insider knowledge. They know how you really are and how the other person really is when their guard is down, when you're being your true self without the artifice that can surround dating or the dance of attraction.

When you're hungry and you ask this person to bring you a ham sandwich, but they can't find ham, they understand, simply from knowing you so well, that turkey is the right substitute. They know your standards well enough to understand what will ensure your needs are met even if your first choice isn't available. They know what characteristics are on your list and know the difference between compromise and settling.

They also know the glue that will bind you together. What is the glue? Maybe it's your family connections, your backgrounds, your education, or your hobbies. Even similar heartbreaks can become the glue that binds. You may have shared some kind of horrific experience, and it's the trauma of that experience that creates the unbreakable bond.

Unfortunately, the days of *Bridgerton*-style balls and coming-out seasons are over. That style of matchmaking, for the majority of us, doesn't exist unless you rely on some sort of computerized algorithm. As much as we may want the opportunity to see a room full of eligible men and women all bent on finding a match, with all their positive and negative attributes on full display, that is not going to happen in this day and age. And we should remind ourselves that in those times, love was the last consideration when making a match.

To be seen, the eligible singles needed to prepare. Preparation is the one thing that is consistent with the process of dating today. These maidens didn't just come out. They stopped eating to lose weight, spent a bunch of money on a wardrobe, tightened their corsets as much as possible, learned who was eligible, which titled men were single, and how much money and property potential suiters had so they could set their sights on the guy with the most wealth. Meanwhile, the mothers were busy telling their daughters what to eat and what to wear and giving instructions because finding a "successful" match reflected on the whole family. Her match, ultimately, would hopefully elevate the family in the elite society. We'll talk more about preparation in the next chapter.

The blatant financial motivations of centuries-old practices are not what I'm talking about when it comes to matchmaking. That said, a matchmaker should operate with the intent of helping two people find each other and build a life together.

Sometimes, despite all the efforts, some women start to feel like the spinster in *Bridgerton*, the one who simply couldn't negotiate a match and ends up growing old while all the young ladies around her get married off. Such women can start to feel like the stepsisters in *Cinderella*. Their feet don't fit the slipper, so they're left with the threat of spinsterhood hanging over their heads.

The truth is, there is nothing *wrong* with being single or not having children. So stop worrying about it. Stop focusing on your clock. Instead of being a spinster, be single and waiting. Read the next chapter to find out what that means.

WHO WOULD YOU TRUST
WITH YOUR HEART?

Are there people in your life you would trust with a relationship suggestion? Who knows you well enough to recommend a potential mate?

Now revisit your list. If you were going to enlist the help of a matchmaker, what would you tell them are the ten characteristics most important to you?

CHAPTER FOURTEEN
Single and Waiting

wait ('wāt), *transitive verb,* to stay in place in expectation of;
to delay serving (a meal); to serve as a waiter for

noun, a state or attitude of watchfulness and expectancy[36]

What do I mean by "single and waiting"? What does "waiting" really mean?

I can tell you, it doesn't mean sitting around waiting for the pool boy to knock on your door and say, "I'm your husband." For men, your perfect match isn't going to show up on your doorstep in a UPS uniform while she's delivering your PlayStation 5 and say, "Hey, you've been waiting for me."

"Waiting" is a verb, an action word. At court, when there were ladies-in-waiting, it was a high honor to serve the queen or princesses in that manner. To be "in waiting" meant to be at the ready to serve. Even today, Kate Middleton has ladies-in-waiting. If you're a royal, who else are you going to trust with the craziness and frustrations that are bound to be connected to that kind of life?

So when I say "single and waiting," that does not mean being single and idle. Let me put it this way. When you go to a restaurant, a waiter waits on you. It is the waiter's job to take your order, deliver your meal, and ensure your dining experience is a pleasant one. So if you're single and waiting, you're actively working to provide the service or to find the person to which you will deliver your love. Does that make sense?

Sometimes, heartbreak can make us still. Our hearts are crushed from the experience. We are trying to heal, but in our pain, we might say, "I don't want to do this ever again in my life."

It's understandable, but it's also the worst possible time to give up. You allow that situation, that heartache, to solder your feet to the floor. It paralyzes you. And if that happens, you really are single. In fact, that frozen feeling means you are not ready. For whatever reason, if you're frozen, you aren't ready to be found, let alone find anyone yourself. And that's okay. Heartache takes time to heal. But you need to allow yourself to heal and not let the wound fester.

If you're single and waiting, you're not hibernating in your home, waiting for someone to come along to save you or bring some kind of meaning to your life.

The scripture that comes to mind is, "... and his interests are divided. And the unmarried or betrothed woman is anxious about the things of the Lord, how to be holy in body and spirit. But the married woman is anxious about worldly things, how to please her husband" (1 Corinthians 7:34, ESV).[37]

I told you in the last chapter about watching the show *Bridgerton*. The young women in Regency-era England didn't just show up at the balls and operas. They had to prepare. They went on diets, acquired new wardrobes, and gathered background information on potential targets. Mothers watched over the efforts because a good match elevated the family in the elite hierarchy.

Today, people who are single and waiting are preparing themselves for something better. They are getting therapy, eating better, and working out. They are working on their mental and financial health. They are ready to connect their life with someone else's. That is what waiting is. Like that waiter in the restaurant, they are preparing to serve up their love to the right person.

Single and waiting should mean you are alone but preparing yourself for something greater. Single and waiting means you aren't in despair, bitter, or depressed because you are single. Single and waiting means you know you're worth finding.

There are some crazy people, especially in the African American community, who think being single is some kind of curse. When we get together, there's always the aunt who asks why you're still single. Or there's the group of people at church who discuss all the single people and express their opinions about why this or that person is still single. Most of the reasons aren't positive.

It might be easy for me to observe this since I am a happily married woman, but I find it ironic that being single gets such a bad rap. Many of those who criticize single people are the ones who are married and miserable—like the way I felt when I wrote my previous book, *Death of the Angry Black Woman.* It is especially during certain customs, such as marriage rites, baptisms, or family gatherings, when the adults do what the adults do while the kids are running around like crazy. This is when singleness is discussed and judged and often labeled as bad. Single people are subjected to quiet—and sometimes not-so-quiet—disapproval.

Instead of viewing being single as something terrible, we should view it as preparation. You don't know when you will find your love, or where you will find them. It could be on the subway, on a plane in the seat next to you, at the grocery store, or while you're taking a walk in your neighborhood. We don't know when it will happen, and we don't know when we will be fully prepared for it. You have no way of knowing when or how your search will end. But if you're single and waiting, you are ready to recognize when these things are happening for you.

I know I'm being repetitive, but repetition is the mother of learning; so I'm gonna say it again. Y'all are sleeping under the same blue sky as your needle. You just haven't met them yet.

Like in the restaurant, even if you don't tip your waiter, he is still going to do the work because that is the job. Even if one connection doesn't work, to be single and waiting means you understand that there will be misses and spills, but you wipe them up and move on because you know something greater is coming. You are waiting, you're single, and you're ready because you know a fine dining experience is about to be delivered to you.

Don't listen to the naysayers who look down on you or criticize you for being single and waiting. It's not a curse, it's not a death sentence, and it's not damnation. Be confident in the knowledge that you are preparing yourself for your fit. You are extending yourself into places you've never been before, whether through travel, trying new restaurants, or picking up new hobbies.

Greatness is something that requires an investment of preparation. Even the most talented artists and athletes have to practice and perfect their skills, or they will never reach the greatness they are capable of. If your thing is to have a great body, you have to sculpt and watch what you eat and spend a great deal of time and energy on creating that perfect physique you aspire to. Waiting is not a spectator sport.

Single and waiting means you are preparing your mind and body and soul to recognize that fit when you find it. Your self-discovery will reveal the things inside you that are worthy of admiration and the characteristics that make it easier for you to love yourself. Once you love yourself, it will be easier for people to see those worthwhile things in you.

After that, your match is up to God. Your wait is for the time when two individuals who are right for each other collide. Being single is not a curse. Waiting is not a bad thing. If you continue to prepare yourself for something, you will find something. What that something is, is between you and God and your eyes and your heart. It's just as the Bible says. Faith and works go hand and hand, right?

You have to work on yourself and that may mean, to you, that you need to work on your faith. You need to put some work in to discover the very thing you've been looking for.

WHAT PREPARATIONS
ARE YOU MAKING?

Think about the things you believe you need to do when preparing to find your perfect fit. List the **improvements you think you need to make** before you will be ready to find love. Consider discussing your list with a close friend. **Do they agree that these things are important?** Also, do you see any value in seeking professional help regarding your improvements?

Example: I don't think I will be ready for a serious relationship until I can get my finances in order.

For the Christian readers of this chapter, 1 Corinthians 7:34 (ESV) "… and his interests are divided. And the unmarried or betrothed woman is anxious about the things of the Lord, how to be holy in body and spirit. But the married woman is anxious about worldly things, how to please her husband."[38]

What have you discovered about yourself?
What things have you discovered you are capable of?

CHAPTER FIFTEEN
Dumpster Diving

(IMDb) *Extreme Cheapskates:* Reality TV/TV Series (2011–2014):
"Exploration of people who go to remarkable lengths
to save money for themselves and their families"
—IMDb.com[39]

I love watching reality TV, maybe because my life sometimes feels like a reality TV show. One of my favorites was *Extreme Cheapskates*, a show about people who went to extraordinary lengths to save money. I'm not talking about penny-pinching or being good at saving money. These people were obsessed with keeping it in their pockets. For example, some of these folks would buy two-ply toilet paper and then pull the layers apart to double their supply. I mean, these people were not normal.

I'll never forget one woman who was very intelligent and highly educated with multiple degrees. She presented herself very well and looked perfectly normal. You would never know she had any weird quirks, but when it came to saving money, she would literally wade into garbage.

Earlier, we talked about your need to eat your wings and shut up. Why? Because when you're out on a date, you need to be in receive mode while you gather your data. I told you to use your mouth for eating, not for talking and revealing everything about yourself.

Now back to our overeducated, frugal woman on the reality show. She would search out good restaurants and then wait until they closed. After closing time, she'd go around the back, looking for their dumpsters. She would literally climb into their dumpsters and pull out the things she thought *looked* good. Old vegetables, old fruit, and all kinds of garbage. Then she would hold dinner parties, inviting a bunch of her friends over, and serve them this food that she had neatly displayed. She'd lay it out all nice, wiped off and cleaned up, not letting her friends know they were eating trash.

Now, I know there is a movement of people out there who dumpster dive because they find the waste of food in this country appalling. There are some people who consider dumpster diving a way of life. But those folks don't serve their friends trash without telling them what they're eating. Those people aren't driven to dumpster diving out of an addiction to saving money. Their efforts are more about calling attention to food waste, and I don't blame them.

But that is not what this woman was doing. In reality, she was serving herself and her friends things that were potentially toxic. She didn't know why that food had been thrown out, if any of it might be contaminated, hadn't been refrigerated properly, or was infected with E. coli. She overlooked the potential toxicity of the food because her addiction to saving money minimized those risks for her. Worse, she never gave her friends the opportunity to opt out of her craziness. It's one thing to make that decision for yourself. It's another thing to hide that information from your friends and fool them into thinking their gourmet meal is legitimate.

What does this have to do with dating?

You've gone on several dates. You are seeing a plethora of people, sifting through the rubble to find your fit and working to discover the things in you that are worth searching for. While out on dates, you're gathering data while eating your wings and paying attention to your list. But now you're probably tired and frustrated. It's the holidays, and you're about to go back to your mama's house where everybody is going to be asking about you still being single and making comments about your clock ticking. You've got holiday parties to go to. You know you're either going with girlfriends or a group of male friends, or you're showing up alone, *again.* The new year is right around the corner—and speaking of clocks, you're so sick of thinking about that clock striking midnight yet again, knowing you won't have anyone to kiss.

But now is not the time to go dumpster diving!

What I'm saying is, no matter how tired you are of the search, how deeply you've mined that rubble, or how desperate you are to find your fit, do not go into that dumpster and search through that poisonous mess. It's too easy to get wrapped up in the damaging, toxic relationships you tossed into the dumpster before. Your fatigue and frustration will suddenly make the behaviors you didn't find acceptable before a bit more tolerable, and you'll start viewing them in a different light.

> DON'T ALLOW YOURSELF TO FEEL SO DESPERATE IN YOUR
> SEARCH FOR HAPPINESS THAT YOU ARE WILLING TO CONSUME
> GARBAGE WHEN IT'S SUPPOSED TO BE THROWN OUT.

I may sound like a rapper when I say this, but dumpster diving can be detrimental to your search. Remember, we talked about standards in To Settle. You could change or, in effect, lower or heighten your standards at any time, but you have to be careful that you're not changing them to accept behavior that you know is detrimental to you just for the sake of shortening your search. Don't search through your red-flag list or change your standards to accept toxic behavior that is not good for you even if you're still drawn to it.

You did the right thing by creating and checking your list, but after some time, you may start to try to convince yourself that a particular behavior is healthy for you, even though when you were clearheaded and not leaning toward giving up, you knew it wasn't. You had that behavior on your red-flag list, but somehow, the loneliness makes you think that red-listed thing isn't so bad. Or you think you're saving yourself from the heartbreak of loneliness, so you begin to change yourself, to customize your needs to fit whatever it was you found in that dumpster.

You know that is never going to work.

You know your ex is not good for you. But you're so frustrated, and you really think you'd like to have a date for that holiday party, so you end up going back to something you know is not good for you. Maybe the holiday party is just the excuse you use because you're feeling so alone and demoralized with finding your fit that you convince yourself you can handle the toxicity you know is buried deep in that old relationship.

I've never said finding your fit is going to be quick. This is going to take time. No matter how long it takes, you cannot allow your impatience to drive you to dumpster diving.

ACCORDING TO A RECENT STUDY OF MORE THAN 3,500 RELATIONSHIPS FROM AROUND THE WORLD, AFTER MORE THAN NINE MONTHS OF A BREAKUP, ONLY 15 PERCENT OF THE COUPLES GOT BACK TOGETHER AND STAYED TOGETHER; 14 PERCENT GOT BACK TOGETHER AND BROKE UP AGAIN, AND 71 PERCENT DID NOT GET BACK TOGETHER.[40]

Why go through all that time and trouble only to come out of the rubble with the kinds of characteristics you know don't work for you? Dumpster diving is bad for everyone. You keep on diving in there, and eventually, you'll end up at the bottom of the barrel surrounded by the kinds of behaviors you've been running away from for a while—maybe as far back as childhood. Behaviors like the controlling, sour, unsupportive, toxic, unhealthy, or abusive nonsense you put on your red-flag list for a reason. You would never put these things on your desired list, but your impatience is making you think all you need to do is brush the issues off and arrange them on a nice plate, and then you'll be good to go.

I know it will sometimes feel as if you're searching for a unicorn or leprechaun or some other mystical creature that only exists in fantasies. I know you're digging through the rubble of life and searching your heap, and you think you will never find what you're looking for. If you've created a list of characteristics that are realistic and important to you, of course, it's going to be hard to find.

IF YOU HADN'T SPENT TIME NEEDING SOMEONE WHO
IS UNIQUE AND SPECIAL AND MADE JUST FOR YOU,
YOU NEVER WOULD HAVE TOSSED THAT INAPPROPRIATE
RELATIONSHIP IN THE DUMPSTER IN THE FIRST PLACE.

Inside that dumpster are things you would never consume, people you would never get involved with or give a second thought. These are people with characteristics that, for you, are toxic. Still, when you get desperate enough, you try to brush them off and make them look acceptable. The predictable outcome is that it causes you internal pain, and you and everyone around you knows it's not good for you.

That relationship, that characteristic was in the trash in the past for a reason.

You only dug it up, cleaned it up, and tried to mask it as something healthy for you when you knew all along that it wasn't because you got impatient.

Ditch the dumpster-diving mentality. If you tossed it away once, chances are it's toxic, it's trash, and it won't last. What's in that dumpster? Things that are never going to be treasure, and I'm sure you've already said at least once that you would never dig them up again. Yet you climbed in the trash again and pulled up someone who never valued you, or you dug up the abuser, the manipulator, the narcissistic personality, the liar, the cheat, the unchangeable characteristics you identified before and that you know are still there. The toxins in that relationship made you gain or lose weight. Your hair might have fallen out, or your health deteriorated, or your self-esteem suffered. You lost a job, got evicted, or suffered from depression, and perhaps you did things you never would have imagined you were capable of doing. All of this because you so desperately wanted to be loved; you somehow made scraping the bottom of the dumpster acceptable. There was a time when you found the strength to get rid of that toxicity. So don't pick it up again.

This is a fresh start. This is how you are going to find your needle in the haystack. Part of that search means you won't be distracted by the garbage you find along the way because you know you're on the search for treasure. Most relationships end for a reason, and if you think about it clearly, you can identify the toxic things that happened that made you toss the relationship in the dumpster and walk away in the first place. Do some people deserve a second chance? Sure. But you know what's good for you and what isn't. It's better to just avoid the dumpsters. Avoid the stink.

In the book of Proverbs, it says, "Like a dog that returns to his vomit is a fool who repeats his folly" (Proverbs 26:11, ESV).[41] Dumpster diving is returning to your folly, returning to your vomit. It happens when you're the most frustrated, the most impatient, and the most vulnerable. You're just tired of being alone. That fatigue is dangerous, and so is dumpster diving. That fatigue makes you look for what is easy, but all it does is set you back much further than ever.

BACK AWAY SLOWLY

What characteristics do you think belong in the dumpster? What characterizes someone you would immediately **disqualify as dating** material?

Example: Someone with a history of partner abuse.

CHAPTER SIXTEEN
Unique You

People often say that "beauty is in the eye of the beholder," and I
say that the most liberating thing about beauty is realizing that you
are the beholder. This empowers us to find beauty in places where
others have not dared to look, including inside ourselves.
—Selma Hayek[42]

O n one of our trips to the park, my mother and my aunts
were busy talking about life and what was going on in their
worlds, exchanging the latest news. We kids wanted to
hang out with them. We knew they were talking about interesting
things, and we wanted to be there to hear it. In our parlance, we
wanted the "T," meaning we wanted them to spill the tea, or more
explicitly, we wanted to hear the latest gossip.

Well, our mother wasn't entertaining that. Kids didn't need to
be up in any grown-up business. So Mom was smart. She pointed
in the direction of a field of clover and said, "Find me a four-
leaf clover."

What did we do? We lay on our bellies in the clover, making
it a game to come up with something that resembled the four-leaf
clover she requested. We were entertained by the search, and as a
bonus to my mom, we spent all that time out of her hair.

As for my kids, when I wanted some time to myself to read or what have you, I would tell them to go find me a rainbow lizard. Of course, there's no such thing as a rainbow lizard, but as long as I had them engaged in finding the impossible, I was able to have more time for myself.

There may not be rainbow lizards, and there may not be many four-leaf clovers, but we search for them anyway. We do it because it may not be completely impossible to find them, and more importantly, what if you're the lucky one who does? In order to find these things, you have to look hard because they are unique. One of a kind. You have to look hard for them because they are rare.

"LOVE TAKES OFF THE MASKS THAT WE FEAR WE CANNOT LIVE WITHOUT AND KNOW WE CANNOT LIVE WITHIN."
—JAMES BALDWIN[43]

If you let yourself believe in the world of endless possibilities, think about the unique possibilities you look for in others. More importantly, in the world of endless possibilities, what are the unique possibilities you offer? What about you is unique?

It's the kind of question you might get on a first date. "Tell me something unique about yourself." What would you say?

Let me tell you, it's important to know this about yourself. What is unique about you sets you apart in the world and is exactly what someone is searching for. There's a reason to keep digging because there isn't another needle like you. You are worth continuing the search for because they haven't found the unique you yet.

The unique part of you isn't just distinctive and rare. It's also appealing. Since it's nearly impossible for you to anticipate what quirky thing about you is attractive to someone else, you have to list everything that is unique.

Yes, I said *list*. It's time to create a list of the unique things about you. This list will encompass the endless possibilities of you. It will include things you may not have considered before. I'm not talking about your athleticism, your beautiful hair, your singing voice, or your virtuosity on the piano. We're talking about the things that are not obvious, the things that are so hidden, even you aren't fully aware of them.

Beauty is in the eye of the beholder, meaning I may look at something and see chaos. You could look at the exact same thing and see something extraordinary. We're working on our list of things we are looking for in a mate, and we're updating it and changing things as we go along because it is a living document. As we learn things about the searching process and about ourselves, our list continues to change.

What we're talking about here are the special things about you that might appear on someone else's list.

> TRUST ME. THERE ARE THINGS ABOUT YOU THAT
> SOMEONE ELSE WILL FIND SPECIAL AND UNIQUE.
> YOU PROBABLY DON'T EVEN KNOW WHAT THEY ARE.

To your siblings, your laugh might be irritating. To someone else, it might sound like music. An old boyfriend might have found your love of animals something he couldn't stand. To someone else, though, your love of small, furry creatures might be beautiful and endearing. You might think that you are clumsy and awkward. To someone else, the way you move might be quirky and charming. Your coworkers could find your ability to keep things organized a useful—but annoying—thing around the office. To someone else, your orderly mind is sexy and appealing in ways you never knew.

Have you ever explored the ins and outs of your personality, your quirks, your habits, or the kinds of things that spark others' interests? Understanding your unique traits, good or bad, is what sets you apart from everyone else in the dating pool. There is the old story of the model who was told to have the gap in her teeth fixed. The model said no because her smile, including the gap, is what makes her unique; it separates her from everyone else in the pool. The very thing one modeling agency despises might be exactly the look someone else wants.

It's perfectly normal for you not to know what your unique but appealing—maybe even weird—thing is. For some of us, it's easy.

Trust me, I am one of the most quirky, peculiar, weird people you will come across. I embrace my uniqueness.

Some unique qualities you have could be what someone else is going to love. You need to know what they are. So I need to you list them. We may as well call this a living document since it's going to take you a while to look inside yourself and find and acknowledge all your quirks. Feel free to add to your list as you continue your self-discovery.

I'm not talking about confessing you were just released after serving twenty years in prison, although that's certainly something that should be shared. I mean, it might be interesting to share that you have a garage full of artistic projects or that you have expertise in growing orchids.

A lot of people know I love music. One thing they don't all know is that deep inside me is a comedian. I use humor to attract others, and getting a laugh makes me stand out. I used to be a bit of a conspiracy theorist and could talk about the ins and outs of a bunch of them, which made it easy to strike up conversations. And when I worked at a large stock brokerage company, it was easy to have long discussions about the markets and other financial topics. That knowledge made me unique.

My husband tells me that intelligent conversation is a big turn-on for him. He is a true sapiosexual. I will talk more about sapiosexuality in the upcoming chapter. For now, let's just say the idea that men are only attracted to physical appearance is not true.

If you're heading out into the dating world, it never hurts to be well-read, to pay attention to what's going on in the world, and to expand your knowledge base. An easy exchange, shared knowledge, and mutual interest can mean you are the person who is remembered the next day. It could be the thing that makes you stand out.

When you know and understand your quirkiness, it can be a topic of conversation. It might be that thing you say when you're in one of those go-around-the-room-and-share sessions. "Hi, I'm Jameliah Gooden, I'm a Gemini, and the unique thing about me is [fill in the blank]."

Difference attracts for many reasons. Uniqueness attracts because it may be rare, it's interesting, and it makes you stand out. The unique thing about you makes you worthy of finding. Perhaps that unique thing about you is what will spark the conversation you and your partner haven't had but need to have.

THE BIG QUESTION

How would you answer the question "Tell me something unique about you?" What are you most proud of? What makes you interesting?

CHAPTER SEVENTEEN
A Sister Gotta Eat

type ('tīp) *noun,* a particular kind, class, or group; something distinguishable as a variety; a member of an indicated class or variety of people; a typical and often superior specimen[44]

Between my husband and me, we have eight children. Collectively, I am part of a blended family of ten. I never expected to have a family so large. I also never expected to be so proud and happy to have all of these children to love. I am so very proud of them.

One day, my twenty-three-year-old daughter, a recent college graduate—again, so proud!—called me to talk about her dating life. She was about to go out on a dinner date but confessed, "Mom, he's really not my type."

My response was, "A sister gotta eat!"

"What?"

"You gotta eat, don't you?"

And my daughter replied, "You're right."

This may be hard for you to wrap your head around. Even if you think someone isn't your type, camaraderie and fellowship are key. It's not about the food. It's about being with someone, conversing, and exploring. Fellowship.

How many times have you turned down a dinner invitation because you assumed the person who asked you out wasn't your type? Now I'm not saying that you have to accept every invitation you get. You have to be open to the fact that you have an idea of who and what your type is. You have your list, and you know better than anyone what it is you like and are looking for.

WHAT YOUR TYPE IS AND WHAT YOU THINK
YOU LIKE MAY NOT BE WHAT YOU NEED.

The very thing you need may be packaged in a way that gives you the impression he is not your type.

It's a bit tricky, but we're not talking about standards or settling or even compromise. We are talking about type and whether you can easily assess type without knowing someone. Even if you can know your potential date's type, how do you know exactly what type is best for you? What if I said you can program your mind to think a particular type is what is right for you because you're attracted to some easily seen characteristic? Perhaps musicians are your type, or you're attracted to guys who look a bit nerdy, or you've always been drawn to athletes. We grow accustomed to these types because it's been our routine, and it's worked for us before.

Or—let's be honest—you are attracted to a specific type because they make your heart go pitter-patter. They turn you on sexually because of their outward appearance, their particular build, their familiar way of speaking. We need to be open to the fact that these immediate turn-ons may not necessarily be the only things that can turn you on. How do you know if you don't give other options a chance?

We've already talked about dating as a way to gather data. I told you to eat your wings and shut up so that you can gather the data your date is providing for you. But what makes you accept the invitation for that date in the first place? If the invitation comes from someone who isn't your type, how will you gather the data on that person if you aren't willing to step beyond your familiar type?

A good meal, coupled with some good conversation and some laughs, could reveal something to you that was hidden so deep in the crevices of your mind and heart, you never would have found it unless God introduced that someone to you.

Scripture says, "Delight yourself in the Lord, and he will give you the desires of your heart" (Psalm 37:4, ESV).[45] This means God knows what's in your heart, and you don't. Sometimes, God will look into the chambers of your heart because there are things impossible for you to see yourself. He says, "I will give you the desires of your heart," meaning he has to introduce you to something, and over dinner, you just might say to yourself, "This person is all right."

I think some people have picked up this book because they really want to find love, but they really don't know what they need. Not really knowing means you need to be ready for the idea that that needle will prick you when you least expect it. That needle will find you before you find it. Then, suddenly, you'll think the search was easy, assuming that moment when the needle found you happened out of luck or because you just stumbled upon it.

It's like when you're getting ready for bed and you stub your toe on the bedpost. You know the bedpost is there. You've walked by it at night hundreds if not thousands of times, but in the dark, you're still not quite sure where the bedpost is until you mash your toe into it. Then you *know* you've found something.

When we are deep into our search, and we don't know what we need, that match has to find us.

Go on that dinner date. Eat the wings and shut up and gather your data. You don't have to accept every invitation, but it doesn't hurt to give someone who isn't your type a chance because a sister gotta eat! A brother gotta eat.

One piece of advice I like to give is, when it's the first time out with someone, whether they are your type or not, go Dutch for the entire evening. You pay for your meal, and I pay for mine. If things work out, no one feels they are under any obligation to do anything else. You are free to come to an understanding as to whether you're going to do it again.

I'm talking to you folks who immediately go to the lobster side of the menu. That shouldn't be what it's about, and ordering the most expensive thing and then expecting him to pay for it gives him some data you may not want him to have.

If there's a second date, who pays can be up for debate. And ladies, we are in a new society. You shouldn't expect that he will pay every time. If it's your idea, you pick up the tab.

Regardless of who pays, sister, you gotta eat. What if you accept that invitation, and you decide over the salad course that this person who isn't your type is amazing? He may not be the man you marry, but he could be an amazing friend. What if he's not your type but you decide you want to know as much about him as you can? Over one meal, you might realize there are hidden qualities in that person that could be good for you.

I'm not gonna lie. The first impression I had of my husband when we finally met face to face was horrible! I'm not kidding; it was bad. I said, "Nah! This ain't gonna work! No, thank you."

We had been video chatting daily for weeks, spending hours and hours on the phone. When I was booked to minister at a conference in Jacksonville, Florida, where he lived, we knew this was the perfect opportunity to finally meet in real life. After driving from Charlotte, North Carolina, I arrived to my hotel very late, but we'd both been excited to finally meet, so we didn't care that it was three in the morning. He was there waiting to meet me.

I admit I was tired, and my judgment may have been skewed by the long drive, but when we first greeted each other and I saw that he was wearing patent leather shoes, I was shocked. I'm like, patent leather shoes? Is that a church shirt? What does he have *on*? I mean, he was just a mess!

But something inside me kept pulling me to him. We had spent hours and hours on video chats and this man in the patent leather shoes did not seem like the same man I had been talking to. Something wasn't right. This man had been in my family for years—there had to be something going on to explain why my first impression of him in person was such a mess. The next day, we had a dinner date. Normally, after that first impression, I would have tried to get out of it, but something told me I needed to see him again. I really didn't care what we were gonna do, I just knew we had to meet. And over that dinner, something about him pulled at me through our conversation and the time we spent laughing together.

ISN'T THAT THE MOST BEAUTIFUL PART OF DATING? WHEN YOU MAKE THAT GREAT DISCOVERY. ONE HOUR BECOMES TWO. TWO HOURS BECOME THREE. THREE HOURS CAN BECOME A LIFETIME.

The truth is, you don't know. You think you do, but you don't know your type.

So if someone asks you to have a meal, and your first reaction is to say no, I suggest you give it some consideration. If it feels right, say yes and go Dutch. You may be at the stage in life where you may think twice about passing up a good meal. Consider the way you've always done things. Consider that it may be time to try something else. Go into the date thinking of it as an opportunity to discover something about them and, maybe, something about you too. Maybe you'll come up with a better understanding of what you've been searching for all along.

TAKE A SECOND LOOK

Have you had a disastrous first date? How did you turn it around?
If you didn't, how could the disaster have been avoided?

CHAPTER EIGHTEEN
Words Matter

sapiosēxūal (sa-pe-o-sek-sh(-)w l) *adjective,*
of, relating to, or characterized by sexual or
romantic attraction to highly intelligent people.

noun, a person who finds intelligence sexually
attractive or arousing, so much so that they consider
it to be the most important trait in a partner [46]

I'm going to share a personal story because this topic is important to me, and I think it perfectly illustrates what I hope you take away from this chapter.

I will never forget the time I went on a date with the man who would eventually be my children's father. At the time, it was still relatively early in our dating life. I was still collecting data, still deciding whether this man was my fit.

We were at The Pink Teacup, a restaurant in Brooklyn. I'd spent some time on myself that night and had gotten all dolled up. I love putting on makeup, and that night, I'd paid particular attention to my face, really wanting to look good for our night out. Now remember, this is my truth. *My* truth. My story. I sat across the table from him, and he said, "You put your face together very well."

I replied, "Thank you. Thank you very much."

He gestured with his hands near his face. "That little sparkly stuff on your face—that's nice."

"Thank you," I said.

By this time, I'm feeling happy. I'd spent extra time on my face, wanting it to look perfect. Not only was I proud of the look I'd achieved, but I was also happy he had noticed and appreciated it. I'm thinking, *This is a man who is willing to notice the small things and to tell me he appreciates my extra efforts.* Who wouldn't want a man who does that?

Then he picked up his glass of water. "I ought to throw this in your face," he said.

Cue the loud, scratchy sound as the needle falls off the record. I didn't know if it was meant as a joke. I didn't know if he meant to hurt me. He'd noticed that I'd obviously spent a lot of time and energy on my makeup, and his reaction was to tell me he wanted to ruin it. Of course, I was hurt. There was no comeback or explanation he could give me that would explain the need to crush my feelings like that.

When I got home from the date, I told my mother I never wanted to see him again. When I told her the whole story, she convinced me to give him another chance. And I did. I ended up giving that man a percentage of my life. We produced two beautiful, amazing children, but the relationship eventually ended in divorce.

The point is, words make something, and words can break something.

The common saying is that beauty is in the eye of the beholder, and on this, I agree. The eyes judge external beauty. What the eyes see is what lures us, what sparks our appetites and desires. The simple vision of someone can make our entire body respond.

While beauty is in the eyes of the beholder, words have the ability to capture and reveal the heart. You know I'm right. What comes out of the mouth can override whatever feelings your eyes may have generated. You can be looking at someone who is stunning, handsome, beautiful, the most attractive person you've seen in a long time. As soon as they start to talk, however, their inner nature is revealed.

You begin to see that your eyes may not be the best judge of character because what your eyes told you may be distorted. The words shatter the very image of what sparked your desires when you initially observed that beauty.

Picture your needle now. It's long and has a point on the end. The eye is where something goes through it and comes out. Let's imagine that the eye of your needle is a mouth.

I've said this before, but I repeat things when they are important. You have to be mindful of what comes out of your mouth, what things you say. I'm not saying you should walk on eggshells or try to be something or someone you're not. I am saying you need to be attentive about what comes out of your mouth.

You've got two ears, two eyes, two nostrils. You have one mouth. Communication is going to make or break your relationship. If you don't know how to converse, learn how. This is something that can be taught and learned.

"WORDS ARE SINGULARLY THE MOST POWERFUL FORCE AVAILABLE TO HUMANITY. WE CAN CHOOSE TO USE THIS FORCE CONSTRUCTIVELY WITH WORDS OF ENCOURAGEMENT, OR DESTRUCTIVELY USING WORDS OF DESPAIR. WORDS HAVE ENERGY AND POWER WITH THE ABILITY TO HELP, TO HEAL, TO HINDER, TO HURT, TO HARM, TO HUMILIATE, AND TO HUMBLE."

—SPIRITUAL LEADER, YEHUDA BERG[47]

Oftentimes, you need to spend time outside of your usual circle to understand how people who are not in your circle hear your words.

Love has a language that has nothing to do with how you look. What you say, how you say it, and how you convey it must be understood. You both need to be comfortable in the knowledge that you have an ability to communicate with each other.

It is what people hear from your mouth that tells them how you expect to be treated. You use your mouth as a defense mechanism to tell others where your line is. It's the mechanism you use to make people understand you. Your ability to communicate plays a major role in finding your fit, finding that true needle in the haystack you've been searching for.

For a lot of us, the gift of gab—which can really be a gift—is what first connected us to the people we love. I am truly grateful for having an ability to communicate. I've told you before that my husband is a sapiosexual. The term, sapiosexuality, is fairly new, but the concept has been around forever. Sapiosexuality is when people are aroused or attracted to others who have the ability to engage them in stimulating conversation. They like people who can talk to them about a wide range of topics. They are attracted to people who communicate well. A deep and engaging conversation is what brought me my true love. I thank God for my ability to talk.

So the sapiosexual is wooed by your words and couldn't care less what you look like. We live in a society where everything is stuffed, fluffed, and inflated. If that's your cup of tea, sip it.

For some people, though, the attraction is in your words. Can you keep someone engaged with what you say? Can you keep someone connected in conversation?

The biblical reference says, "So we do not lose heart. Though our outer self is wasting away, our inner self is being renewed day by day" (2 Corinthians 4:16, ESV).[48]

That scripture means that beauty fades. We get older. The physical manifestation of beauty does not last forever, but the beauty we hold on the inside does. How you treat people and being accountable for what you say have nothing to do with what you look like.

I'm not saying external beauty is a bad thing or that it isn't important. I know that for some of you reading this, your beauty is the main device you use to attract others. You've been blessed with beauty, and so you nurture and wield it. There is nothing wrong with that—and lucky you! Just be sure that the time and energy you put into your external beauty matches the time and energy you apply to your internal beauty.

You should work on your internal beauty because as sure as you are born, you will grow old. I look at my husband and know there is no one else in the world I want to grow old with. I know young people don't like to think about growing old, but at some point, maturity has to kick in. It is inevitable.

It is natural for people, especially the young among us, to desire someone attractive. When you get to be a certain age, you've been there, and you've done that. You've got a drawer full of the novelty T-shirts. When you get caught up in the external beauty, sometimes you're blowing your chance to find someone who may not be drop-dead gorgeous on the outside but who has enough inner beauty to last you both a lifetime.

One of my favorite scriptures says, "The beginning of wisdom is this: Get wisdom, and whatever you get, get insight"(Proverbs 4:7, ESV).[49]

Remember, when you are gathering data during your search, you're not only gathering it about the person you are dating, but you are also gaining an understanding of yourself and what you desire. You are discovering what you want, how you want to be treated, what things make you happy, where you want to live, and what you want to do. As you're dating and working on your list—that living document that changes as you learn more and more about yourself—perhaps you make adjustments in the age range of people you will consider. You may reconsider your position on children and whether you'd be comfortable in a relationship that includes a blended family.

No matter what is on your list, an ability to communicate with the person sitting across from you is vitally important. You both need to be reading the same book of life. You both need to be on the same page.

BAD COMMUNICATION CAN CORRUPT LIKE A FUNGUS AND EAT A RELATIONSHIP FROM THE INSIDE OUT. IF YOU AREN'T SHARING A PERSPECTIVE, THAT FUNGUS COULD ROT THE FOUNDATION.

Sometimes you need to call in a coach to help you sort it out. Someone who can help you understand how to communicate with each other. There is no shame in asking for help. How can you get help if you don't ask for it?

When we're talking about communication, don't fall into the trap of feeling as if you have to tell your entire life's story in one setting over the entree. Don't recite your wish list and expectations before you're done with the appetizer. Remember when I told you to eat them wings and shut up? Communication is listening as well as speaking, and when you're speaking, you need to be mindful of your words, what you're saying, and how much you are sharing.

One appropriate verse is, "They make their tongues as sharp as a serpent's, the poison of vipers is on their lips" (Psalm 140:3, ESV).[50]

Another scripture talks specifically about how the tongue can do so much damage: "So also the tongue is a small member, yet it boasts of great things. How great a forest is set ablaze by such a small fire! ... For every kind of beast and bird, of reptile and sea creature, can be tamed and has been tamed by mankind, but no human being can tame the tongue. It is a restless evil, full of deadly poison." (James 3:5, 7–8, ESV).[51]

A restless evil. We know that's right. Watch your words!

When you've found the right needle, the words that needle creates can weave beauty in the fabric of life. Every stitch has a story.

And if every stitch has a story, that story can create a beautiful quilt that will comfort you in every bad situation. Believe it or not, you can find such beauty and comfort in words. When you're dating, someone may have to hear those beautiful and comforting words. What you say will ultimately be what brings that person to think they want to go out with you again. Things you say will make your date feel a certain way. Your comforting words may be exactly what your date is looking for.

And one more thing. This is important and might hurt some feelings. But this is something God taught me years ago, and I'm going to teach it to you because I like you! I love to teach. That's what I've been created to do. That is my purpose in life and one of the things my husband and I have in common. He's a great teacher. Like I said, this may hurt you, but it could also save you a whole lot of heartbreak. Ready? You're going to want to highlight this or capture it in your notes. Get a pen if you have to because here it is.

The people who have the most difficulty finding a relationship are the ones who are selfish. Selfish people are unable to have lasting relationships. I'm not saying they need to stop searching. I am saying that as you work on yourself as you work on finding your fit, selfishness is one of those things that you should invest the time and energy to fix. There's no shame in asking for help. If you think you are selfish, work on that.

"GOOD LORD BOYET, MY BEAUTY, THOUGH BUT MEAN, NEEDS NOT THE PAINTED FLOURISH OF YOUR PRAISE: BEAUTY IS BOUGHT BY JUDGEMENT OF THE EYE, NOT UTTER'D BY BASE SALE OF CHAPMEN'S TONGUES." SHAKESPEARE'S *LOVE'S LABOUR'S LOST*, 1598[52]

Why do I say that? If you're going to find your fit, if you're searching for your needle in the haystack, communication goes both ways. You may be on the search for the perfect needle, but finding someone you think is perfect for you won't be enough. You have to find someone you think is perfect for you who also thinks you are perfect for them. Your needle search is not a solitary activity. There has to be someone on the other side of the table who is just as important as you are in the equation. You're looking for someone who is willing to do the work with you and someone you are willing to do the work for. You won't be willing to do the work you need to do if you're selfish. Your needle search isn't about *you*. Your needle search is about *we*.

CHAPTER NINETEEN
The Interrogation

I have a tendency to sabotage relationships;
I have a tendency to sabotage everything.
Fear of success, fear of failure, fear of being afraid.
Useless, good-for-nothing thoughts.
—Michael Bublé[53]

I never know when God is going to drop an idea into my head. He did that early this morning. The revelation he gave me this morning wasn't for me. It was for all the single women who are searching for their needle to find their fit. Now, I know that there are men searching too, but this is specifically for women because when I tell you this revelation, you will recognize it and know whether this is about you. There may be some men who do this as well, and even if you don't, it doesn't hurt for you to understand what is going on if it happens to you.

Let me start off by saying, in a lifetime, women go through an unbelievable amount of heartache. Most of us can say that we've experienced more heartbreak along this search than we have joy. Men suffer heartache as well, but women—especially women who are on this search for their needle in a haystack—well, they have a long journey ahead of them. People always say you're going to kiss a lot of frogs along the way. That would be fine if we could more easily identify the frogs once we've kissed them.

But I'm speaking more specifically to women now because we can be our own worst enemies. As I've said before, it feels like there is a lot of competition out there for the perfect match, especially for black women, because there *is* a lot of competition out there. That competition sometimes leads us to engage in activities that are not just a bit desperate but truly self-sabotaging. In other words, the perception of competition leads us to do things that hurt us more than help us.

You are reading this book because you are searching for your needle in a haystack, and you're doing it in a way that will make it easier for that needle to find you. Unlike other cultures in which there are matchmakers, we follow the practice of courtship, the get-to-know-you phase, the period of time when we are gathering data, and this is often where things fall apart. Even if you've found the perfect needle, even if the good fit has found you, that self-sabotage thing comes into play.

How do we self-sabotage? I'm going to share some hard truths with you. It's better for me to give you the hard truth here before someone else comes along and fills your head with soft lies. Try to open your heart to hearing the message in this illustration before the defensive walls go up.

In the needle factory, needles are going through a punch press that has been set to a specific standard. In that press, the needles come popping out and travel along a conveyor belt. At the end of the conveyor belt is a quality-control inspector. This inspector tests the needle to ensure the eye is wide enough, the needle is strong enough, and the needle is long enough to fit the exact specifications the factory has set. If the needle doesn't pass the quality-control inspector, a red light goes off, and the needle gets tossed out. The rest of the needles are judged just right, so they get packaged up and head to the stores for you to purchase.

Now, what if some of those needles get inspected a little more closely? They get put through a stress test. The needles are bent and stomped on and twisted just a little more than any of the other needles because this particular inspector just wants to make doubly sure they can handle the tests they've been put through. The problem is, none of the needles are built for that, so they break. They get tossed out. They are deemed unworthy when really, they were put through tests they were never designed for in the first place.

WE NEED TO STOP THE HIGH-POWERED QUALITY INSPECTIONS, LADIES. MOST MEN WEREN'T BUILT FOR THEM.

So God put this thought in my head this morning. I woke up thinking about some of the women I encounter on a day-to-day basis who use this form of self-sabotage. They question, prod, doubt, suspect, and interrogate. For some, it's like a game to see if they can catch a man in a lie and prove their suspicions that he isn't all that he has claimed to be.

Let me give you an example. The first date goes fine. Your conversation is easy; you enjoy each other's company. You think there just might be something to build on. The second date goes better. You're getting to know each other; you're making plans to do other things together. You're thinking about when and if you'll introduce him to your friends. At the end of the date, he tells you he has to go out of town for a few days for work or to visit family. Or you invite him to do something, and he tells you he's unavailable because he's got something else planned. Or he says he wants to let you know that he won't be available for a week or so and will have limited access to his phone.

You were dancing along, feeling great about how things were going, and now he's telling you there's going to be a break for a few days, and you let your imagination go wild. You go into detective mode. You suspect something more is going on. You've spent the last week or two thinking about nothing other than this man. Even though it's only just begun, what you have started with this man is the most important thing going on in your life right now. How can he say he's not going to be available for a few days? What is that about? As soon as you see him again, you start with the questions.

Where did you go? Who was with you? I thought you said you were going with someone else. Didn't you tell me you were going to your mother's house? Were you lying to me? But you told me something else—I saw your social media post. Who were those people in your Instagram photo? I don't think you went where you are telling me you went. How can I trust you? I called you. You didn't call me back. You said you wouldn't have access to your phone but you posted a tweet. And on and on.

Now, don't get me wrong. I know some of you may have been hurt. You may have been lied to. You may have been cheated on. You may even have suspicions that are valid. The problem is, when it's early in a relationship and you barely know each other, suspicion can be like a poison. No one likes to be interrogated. And no one likes their every word pulled apart and scrutinized. You don't even know where this relationship is going.

Remember, you're supposed to be in the period where you are gathering data—and one data point you will find out very quickly is that he hates being interrogated.

Suspicious Minds by Elvis Presley

We're caught in a trap,
I can't walk out,
Because I love you too much, baby.

Why can't you see,
What you're doing to me,
When you don't believe a word I say?

We can't go on together
With suspicious minds (with suspicious minds).
And we can't build our dreams
On suspicious minds.

So if an old friend I know
Stops by to say hello,
Would I still see suspicion in your eyes?

Here we go again
Asking where I've been.
(You can't see the tears are real, I'm crying.)
(Yes, I'm crying.)[54]

Believe me. I get it. You're caught between this feeling that you want to protect yourself by ensuring he is being truthful and the desire to know things he's not willing to tell you simply because you're not there yet. You hardly know each other. When it's early on, there are any number of reasons why he would hold information back or withhold the complete truth.

What if, when he says, "I'm going out of town for a few days and won't be able to communicate," it really means something that is too revealing or complicated to share on a second or third date? Maybe he could have said, "I'm going out of town to help my aunt clean out her house after my uncle died, and I'm doing it because she and my mother don't get along, but I really loved my uncle, and I won't be calling because this will be a very emotional chore for me, and I really don't know where my head will be while I'm there."

He could have told you all that, but at the same time that you are deciding if you trust him, he is deciding if he can trust you with his innermost emotional issues and family drama. Perhaps he fears his family drama so early in a relationship will turn you off. Or what if when he says he couldn't have dinner with you because he already had plans, those plans were to have dinner with an old friend. This was a date he'd made before he met you, and yes, the old friend is an old girlfriend, but she lives out of town, and he's not sure how he feels about her—and he's not sure how he feels about you either. He's torn over whether to share that he's going on a date with an old flame because he doesn't want to ruin his chances with you when everything is so uncertain. He has a right to that uncertainty, doesn't he? Especially so early on in your data-gathering time. So if you ask him to dinner, and he says he has other plans, should that immediately raise suspicions? Should that earn him time in the interrogation room?

We all hate being interrogated. We hate feeling under suspicion, especially in the early days of the courtship. If you are a habitual interrogator, you may find yourself a permanent fixture on the shelf. They will store you in the pile labeled "crazy," "insecure," or "clingy." If you're a man, the labels are "controlling," "stalker," or "domineering." Your continued interrogations may make them feel as if you'll never trust them anyway, no matter what they do. So why be truthful? And, I hate to say it, but why would a partner put a ring on the finger of someone who is unable to trust them?

There are far too many of us who are unable to trust. Like I said, we've been through a lot. Many people blow their opportunities at finding their fit because of their insecurities or the pain of their past.

I SAY THIS ALL THE TIME, AND I WILL SAY IT AGAIN HERE:
DO NOT LET YOUR PAST CRIPPLE YOUR FUTURE.

I get it. People have been hurt. Your antennae are up. You're looking for the red, flashing danger sign. There are many people and situations that have made you suspicious and distrustful and perhaps rightly so. Black women, especially, deal with so much abuse and have so much baggage throughout our lives. We need that self-defense mechanism to ensure we can survive.

I'm not saying you shouldn't use your instincts. When it is time to build a true, lasting relationship, trust will be a major part of that foundation. Trust takes time, and trust is vital, but trust, complete truth, and openness are not immediate.

You can't walk through the door of a relationship expecting to be taken seriously if your habit is to interrogate. No one likes to be interrogated. Men hate it. Women hate it. If you've ever been interrogated, you know that even if you are completely innocent, it makes you feel guilty! An interrogation makes you feel as if there is no positive way the situation will end well because no answer will be sufficient.

If you're just starting to date someone and you're video chatting with them to see where they are and who they are with, that's not a good thing. If you're running around behind them, verifying their story with other people after a couple of dates, they will find out, and they will run in the opposite direction. When you don't know someone, and you are in the getting-to-know-you phase, many things that are perfectly innocent can appear suspicious to those with trust issues. We self-sabotage when we demand full disclosure and full commitment too early, especially when the status of the relationship has not been established.

Now hear me when I say this: many of these trust issues become amplified when people become intimate before they have established that they are in a committed relationship. Let me say that again. Jumping into bed with someone makes the trust issues go off the charts. If you haven't established exactly what that intimacy really means to both of you in terms of the relationship, of course you're going to feel distrustful and used if you weren't both on the same page. If you thought sex meant one thing, and he thought it meant something else, the red lights should be flashing for both of you because you've gone down a rocky road you may not recover from. The opportunity for finding your fit in this instance may have been blown.

I've said it before. If you are coming out of a bad relationship, you probably need to seek help with your trust issues. If you are using interrogation techniques to attempt to protect yourself from further harm, you need to deal with the inner harm that has already been done. If you are someone who has a problem with trust, don't be afraid to get help for that. Now is the time to do that work on yourself so you can be open to the love that will find you when you've searched through the haystack.

WORK ON YOUR TRUST ISSUES BEFORE YOUR INTERROGATIONS DRIVE
AWAY SOMEONE WHO COULD BE YOUR PERFECT FIT.

When you've worked on your trust issues, you can enter the data-gathering stage and go on dates without expectations. When you're going on dates and gathering data, you should also be building trust! If the initial dates lead to something more, that's beautiful. If the initial dates reveal things that aren't for you, perhaps you've at least made a friend. It's important that you relax. Enjoy the journey. God taught me something that I hope to teach you. God taught me I may need to hurt your feelings to save your life.

SELF-SABOTAGE LIKE A BOSS

Many of us self-sabotage our relationships, and we're very good at it. Sometimes we don't even know that we are doing it.

Create a list of ways you self-sabotage your relationships. Once you've created your list, discuss it with trusted friends. Are these the only ways you have self-sabotaged a relationship? Listen to the ways they describe their self-sabotage habits and see if they apply to you. We don't always know when we are self-sabotaging, so ask someone close what they think.

What are some examples of self-sabotage?

- Flirting excessively in front of or even cheating on your partner
- Not returning calls or texts or the reverse, excessively calling and texting
- Criticizing everything they do
- Laughing at them or embarrass them in front of your friends

These are just a few examples. If it's something that would drive you crazy if the situation were reversed, it's probably self-sabotage.

CHAPTER TWENTY
Stop the Cray-Cray

ghosting ('gō-stin), *noun,* the act or practice of abruptly cutting off all contact with someone (such as a former romantic partner) by no longer accepting or responding to phone calls, instant messages, etc.[55]

At one time, I regularly counseled a woman who was in a terrible situation. Just about every day of her marriage, her husband beat her. He would sometimes strike her more than once a day. All day long, she was in fear of being beaten. She would call me all the time. We talked and talked, but no matter what I said, she would never leave him. I finally had to stop counseling her when she came clean, and I finally learned why she stayed with him. It wasn't because of their children or that she was afraid—or even that she didn't have anywhere to go. She told me she stuck with her husband because "The dick is so good."

Please excuse the crass way I've said this, but I'm purposefully repeating her words so you can understand just how shocking it was for me at the time. It was the craziest thing I'd ever heard!

All the time and energy I had poured into trying to help this woman, and the main reason she was allowing herself to be brutalized and to live a hellish life was because of the sex. Obviously, the help she needed went far beyond the religious counseling I was providing her.

As a woman and as a leader and having grown up in a household with domestic violence, it was the most preposterous thing I'd ever heard.

Sex will impair your vision. Sex will throw you off your game. Sex, especially if you're immature, will not allow you to clearly gauge your situation and make informed decisions.

This world is crazy. I'm sure you've heard that before. I mean, people will do and say some crazy things. Sometimes, you have no warning of how absolutely unexpected the craziness can be.

I believe in sharing knowledge because I hate to see people destroyed due to their lack of it. When it comes to relationships, a lack of knowledge can mean you simply don't know what is happening to you. You become blind to reality. So let me help by pulling the wool back from your eyes.

I want you to use your eyes to realistically see that haystack. We've already talked about how you're going to run across a variety of needles. Some of them will have the characteristics you're looking for. Some needles will be rejected because they aren't right for you. I hope and pray that by this time, you are open to finding all types of needles—needles that cross all spectrums of race, class, shape, and size. Somewhere in there is the right needle for you because both you and the person you are seeking are being open-minded about finding the right fit.

ACCORDING TO PSYCHCENTER.COM, ON GHOSTING: THE OTHER PERSON HAS DECIDED TO MOVE ON FOR WHATEVER REASON. ACCEPTING THAT IS MORE IMPORTANT THAN KNOWING WHY. THE GHOST IS ALSO DEMONSTRATING THAT HE OR SHE DOESN'T RESPECT YOUR FEELINGS AND LACKS ESSENTIAL COMMUNICATION AND CONFLICT RESOLUTION SKILLS THAT MAKE RELATIONSHIPS WORK. YOUR FEELINGS ASIDE, CONSIDER WHETHER YOU REALLY WANT A RELATIONSHIP WITH THEM.[56]

Then there are the needles that maybe never should have made their way into that haystack in the first place.

Which brings me to this idea of ghosting.

Ghosting happens when, for whatever reason, one of the people in the relationship cuts the other person off completely, no warning, no explanation, no resolution. It may be a cowardly and mean-spirited way of ending a relationship. It's also something that happens more frequently than we might think.

In the last chapter, we talked about trust and the idea that trust should be present in a relationship before sex becomes a factor. There are probably a lot of you reading this book right now who are nodding your heads. Maybe you've used an app to find a one-night stand. Maybe you've met someone at a bar, and you've gone off and had sex with them right away. Maybe you've gone out on a first date, and instead of taking the time to get to know each other, you tumbled into bed right away.

This kind of tumble is dangerous on so many levels. It's dangerous because you don't know that person's medical history. It's dangerous because you don't know who that person really is or what their true intentions are. They even made a movie about it. Remember *Fatal Attraction*? A married man thought he was having a one-night stand with someone who said that was what she wanted. Turned out, she was completely cray-cray! And his sexcapade brought that cray-cray right into his family's world.

I'm not being judgmental here. I'm a realist, and I'm fully aware that this no-strings kind of sex is what a lot of people do ... or think they do. Sex is rarely no strings. And I'm aware that the chances are slim that you'd ever end up in that kind of *Fatal Attraction* disaster. What is more likely to happen is that you'll be ghosted.

Maybe some of you have been ghosted. Maybe some of you have ghosted someone else. Either way the pendulum swings, ghosting hurts. Ghosting is wrong.

Fatal Attraction, by Paramount Pictures (1987) starring Michael Douglass, Anne Archer, and Glenn Close. Close was nominated for a Best Actress Oscar for her role in the film as the women who would not be ignored. Other Academy Award nominations were for Best Picture, Best Director, Best Screenplay, and Best Editing. It did not take home any of the golden statues. Why do people ghost in the first place?

I know there are all kinds of ideas about sex, sexual freedoms, and sexual adventure. You probably think I'm being old-fashioned or that I'm some kind of prude. Trust me. I am not a prude. What I will say is that if a string of sexual conquests is your goal, this is not the right book for you. Close it. Put it down. You're not ready for this book.

Ghosting happens when one person doesn't want to face the awkward breakup conversation. They don't want to be asked why. They don't want to explain. They just want to walk away. No matter how you look at it, ghosting happens because you put your trust in a person, and they let you down.

In a previous chapter, we also talked about the interrogation, how no one

FATAL ATTRACTION (MOVIE SUMMARY): "FOR DAN GALLAGHER (MICHAEL DOUGLAS), LIFE IS GOOD. HE IS ON THE RISE AT HIS NEW YORK LAW FIRM, IS HAPPILY MARRIED TO HIS WIFE, BETH (ANNE ARCHER), AND HAS A LOVING DAUGHTER. BUT AFTER A CASUAL FLING WITH A SULTRY BOOK EDITOR NAMED ALEX (GLENN CLOSE), EVERYTHING CHANGES. JILTED BY DAN, ALEX BECOMES UNSTABLE, HER BEHAVIOR ESCALATING FROM AGGRESSIVE PURSUIT TO OBSESSIVE STALKING. DAN REALIZES THAT HIS MAIN PROBLEM IS NOT HIDING HIS AFFAIR BUT RATHER SAVING HIMSELF AND HIS FAMILY."[57]

likes to be interrogated, and that interrogation usually happens out of a lack of trust. Having sex too early in a relationship is a good way to set yourself up for the chance of an interrogation later, simply because if you tumbled into bed with one person, isn't there a good chance you'll tumble into bed with someone else?

In church, we talk about the spirit of discernment. The spirit of discernment means having the ability to know right from wrong. Sometimes we need some help to see what is right and what is wrong.

ACCORDING TO A PEW RESEARCH REPORT, YOUNG ADULTS BETWEEN AGES 18 AND 29 ARE THE MOST LIKELY TO GHOST SOMEONE OR TO BE GHOSTED (42 PERCENT). OLDER ADULTS HAVE EXPERIENCED GHOSTING AS WELL, ESPECIALLY THOSE ADULTS WHO PARTICIPATE IN ONLINE DATING. AGES 30–49, 37 PERCENT; 50–64, 21 PERCENT; AND 65+, 14 PERCENT.[58]

What I'm saying is, instead of finding yourself in a position where you might be ghosted, get yourself a ghostbuster!

That may sound funny. We all like a good movie. Obviously, I'm not talking about that kind of ghostbusting.

GET YOURSELF ANOTHER SET OF EYES. ENLIST A FRIEND OR FAMILY MEMBER TO WEIGH IN ON THIS PERSON YOU THINK YOU'RE FALLING FOR BEFORE YOU TAKE THE NEXT STEP AND SLEEP WITH THEM.

We think we're independent and able to make our own decisions, but sometimes, we get so wrapped up in our desire to find someone, we avoid seeing the things that are perfectly visible to others.

One of the book projects I have in mind down the road is called *Dating with Your Clothes On*. I'm going to get to it as soon as I can. Please be patient with me. Until then, I'm going to say something that may not go over so well because of the society we live in, but I care about you, so I'm not going to shy away from it. You're going to hear this from me, though you've probably already heard it from your nana. Take a minute to listen to the crazy lady in the car (if you haven't yet, you should be tuning in to my Car Chronicles each morning), knowing that I'm saying this with all due respect.

Don't jump into bed. Don't have sex right away. Give it time. Do your data mining before you take your clothes off. I'm a pastor, but I'm also a realist. If you're truly looking for that needle, if you're serious about finding your fit, keep your damn clothes on.

When you were eighteen, nineteen, or maybe twenty years old, sex might have been enough to keep you engaged for a while. Sex is not enough to keep someone engaged in an adult relationship.

The minute you introduce sex into the relationship, it interferes with your decision-making. It's almost as if the work of getting to know each other suddenly gets pushed aside and replaced with sexual exploration.

Remember the woman who wanted my help with domestic violence? Once she told me she was willing to stay in an abusive relationship because the sex was so good, I knew there was nothing I could do or say that would help her. More importantly, I knew all the time I'd spent with her had been wasted.

Knowing someone's erogenous zones is not the same thing as knowing they grew up in a household that respected hard work and the ability to make decisions. The way he makes you feel beneath the sheets is not the same as finding out he volunteers in a homeless shelter.

If sex is introduced too early in a relationship, especially if you are immature, it will be as if you are seeing him or her through a completely different set of lenses.

At one time, I was in a relationship where I was being manipulated, but I didn't see it. People tried to open my eyes. "I don't think he's right for you," they said. "He's not a good match for you," they said. When I didn't listen to their sound advice, I was used, abused, and manipulated. This man didn't love me. I paid a heavy price because I didn't listen, and I let sexual gratification blind me to the truth.

That was then. This is now. Trust me on this.

My advice to you is to make it clear from the beginning and have a conversation about what needs to happen before sex will become part of your relationship. Even if you're not having sex, but the idea of sex seems to permeate the relationship, you may become tone-deaf to everything else. If all you're doing is flirting or talking dirty to each other, you are not getting a realistic picture of who he is, nor will he know who you are.

If you really want to find your fit and want a relationship that is mature, solid, and substantial, keep your clothes on, don't steam up the car windows in the driveway, and don't have phone sex. Let all that wait for later when you've both come to a clear understanding of what you both want.

Before you get to a hotel, before he shows you his beautiful house, before you Netflix and chill, you need to come to an agreement about what role sex will play in your early relationship, and you need to speak to your ghostbuster. The last thing you want to happen is to wake up in his bed wondering what just happened. You don't want to be asking yourself why you did that.

My mother used to say, "God takes care of two people. He takes care of babies, and he takes care of fools." I am sure most of the people reading this book have been both. To avoid being the latter, I am putting as much knowledge as I have on the topic within the pages of this book. I don't want you to get hurt. I don't want you to be ghosted. I don't want you to ruin your chance of finding your fit because you were too quick to jump into bed.

If you pay attention to the sexual undertones in the conversation, you will bust the ghost before the ghost busts you.

One final note. While I had to stop counseling the person who felt that sex was more important than her safety, that doesn't mean all domestic violence situations are hopeless. They aren't. If you are in an abusive relationship, get help. If you are in a situation where you are being bullied by a former love interest, stalked in real life or online, don't mess around. Get immediate help. You do not deserve abuse.

KEEP YOUR CLOTHES ON

What needs to happen in your needle search before you are ready to have sex with a new partner?

Example: I need to make introductions and see interactions with my family before I take my clothes off.

GIVE UP THE GHOST

In this chapter, we talked about being ghosted and how hurtful that can be. Have you ever ghosted anyone? If so, why? Have you been ghosted?

Consider ghosting. Discuss this practice with your friends. What is the prevailing feeling about ghosting? Is there a place for ghosting in your needle search?

CHAPTER TWENTY-ONE
R U a Shrew?

> My tongue will tell the anger of my heart,
> Or else my heart, concealing it, will break.
> —Katherina in William Shakespeare's
> *The Taming of the Shrew* [59]

Everyone likes a little Shakespeare, and one of my favorites is *The Taming of the Shrew*. If you're not familiar with this story, Elizabeth Taylor and Richard Burton filmed a version of it in 1967. It won a Golden Globe award that year. Better yet, read the play and you'll get the full flavor of what Shakespeare had to say on the topic.

Anyway, Shakespeare's story is about a woman whose anger and bitterness make her perpetually cantankerous to the point where she is unbearable. The entire story is completely misogynistic and patriarchal, as most of Shakespeare's stories from those times are, but if you can get past all that, there are some interesting things to consider. For example, it's clear that Katherina is very much like a wild stallion who refuses to be broken.

I like to go horseback riding on occasion. Once, it was explained to me that stallions are the most difficult to tame because they have to be broken first. This particular horseman told me if you can't break a stallion, as harsh as it may sound, you ultimately have to shoot it because it's untrainable.

When one watches a wild stallion, especially one who refuses to be broken, it's difficult not to admire them. This is a brave, beautiful creature that is stubborn and willful. They refuse to be told what to do. They battle against it with everything they have, stomping and bucking and fighting until they are completely exhausted.

As Shakespeare's shrew, Katherina is as stubborn as a stallion. We see her rant and rave, fight and claw her way through the story, claiming all the while she will never live under a man's thumb. Her siblings tell her she will be a spinster because no one can stand to be around her and her nasty disposition. It's not until someone takes on the notion of taming her as a challenge that anyone gets close to wading through all the negativity to find the true Katherina.

Sometimes, in singleness, we allow ourselves to get into a shrewlike disposition. Over years of rejection or betrayal, dashed hopes and unrequited feelings, we become angry, bitter, and fearful of being hurt. Above all, we refuse to buckle under and be tamed. Just the notion that someone is trying to break or tame you is enough to send you into a frenzy. Am I right?

No one is telling you that you need to be broken. What I am saying is that you need to be open and approachable to allow yourself to be loved. So let's think about all the things that have occurred throughout your life, your dating experiences and beyond, that hurt you and brought you to this place of anger.

Now here I go with another list. It won't be easy, but let's commit to paper all of the people who hurt you, either through rejection or some other means. You don't have to go into detail. Just a line or two that paints the picture of what happened. You should put names to the people who drove you to your shrewlike nature. Let me give you a few examples: Your best friend stole your high school sweetheart. You caught the love of your life kissing a neighbor. The man you dated for years never remembered your birthday. Someone you cared about finally asked you out and then never showed. Does any of this sound familiar?

You know, when we first start dating, one of the things that attracts us to the other person is how nice they are. That niceness makes us feel a certain way about ourselves and about them. But some of us are not so nice. It's not within our nature to be bright and open and willing to share our innermost self without putting people through challenges and tests to see how much we can trust them. Not only do we not trust, but we also don't keep that lack of trust to ourselves. We challenge and remind others that trust is something that very much needs to be earned.

I'm telling you the Shakespeare story because somewhere there is someone like Shakespeare's Petruchio who is willing to be patient with you and stick with you through the process of being found. Now, mind you, ever'body ain't gon' do this. You hear me? The more difficult you make it, the less likely you will be found. Imagine that needle just burrowing itself deeper and deeper and deeper into that haystack because it is a rare needle.

IT TAKES A SPECIFIC AND SPECIAL INDIVIDUAL TO LOVE YOU PAST YOUR PAIN. WE KNOW THEY NEED TO BE SPECIAL BECAUSE IT'S DIFFICULT FOR EVEN YOU TO LOVE YOU PAST YOUR PAIN.

Think about that.

To find love, you need to love you past your pain. If you could do that, we may not have to talk about being shrewlike in the first place. Do you understand?

In *The Taming of the Shrew*, Petruchio looks at Katherina and sees something greater than what she saw herself. That happens in love. Someone will see past your trauma and see that you really are a gem, a precious thing. It's the hard, crusty things around your beautiful, valuable, and rare heart that cause you to lash out, that make it more difficult for that perfect fit to find the gem.

The dating game is tough. It's not an easy game to play. It can be rough-and-tumble like football. You have some people who trot off the field, and their uniforms are as fresh and clean as when they trotted on the field. Others have turf burns, uniforms that are torn and stained, and even broken limbs. In the dating game, we can be hurt with lingering wounds from past loves, maybe a recent relationship, maybe a divorce, or maybe some other slight. Perhaps you're being shrewlike because as a widow or widower, in your eyes, no one will ever reach the standards at which you held your partner who passed away. Maybe, deep down, you're angry at them for leaving you, even though you know in your heart their passing wasn't their fault.

No matter what you've been through, you have to ask yourself, what is the vibe I'm throwing off? How do people perceive the things I say, the way I respond to others? When you're sitting across from your date—and hopefully eating your wings—is the emotion you're displaying openness? Or do you look skeptical and doubtful? When you make a joking remark, does it sound more like a sharp rebuke? When you're speaking on the phone or responding via text or email, are the things you're saying coming out harsher than you intended?

The person on the other side of that conversation is going to be receiving what you are putting out. What if that person decides it's impossible to ride the stallion?

ARE YOU GOING TO BE THE STALLION THAT CAN BE TAMED?
OR ARE YOU GOING TO BE THE STALLION THAT HAS
TO BE RELEASED BACK INTO THE WILD?

In the quote at the top of this chapter, Kate says if she doesn't let her anger out, it will destroy her. I think sometimes we all feel that way, so angry and frustrated that we have to let it out. The question is, are you unleashing the anger and frustration in the right direction?

Like most of Shakespeare's plays, there are several good lessons to be learned in *The Taming of the Shrew*. In my mind, a major one happens when Kate begins to think she is perceived as being disagreeable because of her own choices. Perhaps she is alone because of her behavior. Maybe you are shrewlike because you're simply not ready. Maybe you're an unbreakable stallion because you're not willing to be vulnerable to the feelings of love that may come your way.

Being single, being alone, can be a real test of character. If you feel alone over the holidays or while attending weddings, funerals, and other events, you likely suffer from loneliness. Certainly, there are single people who are okay with being single at these events, but I suspect if you're reading this book, loneliness is becoming, if it isn't already, very much a factor in your life. Are you broadcasting the pain of being alone? Is your loneliness a badge you are wearing for all to see?

Anger, indifference, loneliness, pain. These are emotions that, when perceived, can give off a feeling that a person is untouchable. These emotions communicate that this is a person who isn't in a position to be tamed or broken. The emotion we radiate may indicate that this is a person who is not ready for love.

Yes, Shakespeare is misogynistic and out of step with the times. All the talk about obeying a husband and being subservient is beyond the pale. One could easily dismiss the play for promoting the idea that a woman is expected to dote on a man, live her life in complete service to a man, or any of the other patriarchal ideas pushed throughout the entire play. But just as we know a woman or a man (men can be shrewlike too) should be in charge of their lives and make their own decisions, they should also be in charge of their readiness for love. There are times we think we are ready for love when we aren't. We've got emotional baggage that is dragging us down, giving off negative vibes, painting us as being suspicious, angry, and overall, not open to receiving love.

One of the saddest things I see is when someone attempts to have a relationship with someone else without understanding the level of pain that person is in. Then, when they are confronted by the fruits of that pain, they end up suffering their own kind of pain. Broken people do break other people.

NO ONE WILL SAVE YOU FROM YOURSELF. EVEN IF A
MAN IS WILLING TO ATTEMPT TO TAME THE STALLION,
IT IS ALWAYS THE STALLION THAT DECIDES IN THE END
IF AND WHEN THEY ARE READY TO BE RIDDEN.

At some point, Kate had to decide if she would let Petruchio love her. He was willing to fight for her, but the decision to be loved was always hers.

People talk about closure and how there can be healing in closure. To an extent, I believe this to be true. There may be times when you don't understand why a particular relationship ended or where it went wrong. Perhaps you should consider going to this person and asking, "What happened here? Where did I mess up?" Take these answers with a grain of salt. Don't be too willing to take on the blame for the relationship failure, but a consistent answer may be a learning tool. It may be hurtful to hear things that past love interests say about you, but it may help in your self-discovery journey.

For example, how do you determine the common denominator in the relationship ending? If each relationship ends with the other person saying the same thing, perhaps that's something you should consider.

I will use myself as an example. In my past, I have often heard, "You don't need a man because you're too strong" as a reason for a relationship ending. If three different people tell you the same thing, it might be time to listen to what the universe is telling you.

I suspect I am not the only modern black woman who has heard this. We are smart, strong, determined, and sometimes give off the impression that we are bulletproof. We go through life demonstrating that we can do anything. Still, I had to sit and think about how my self-sufficiency was perceived by potential love interests. Perhaps it's true that I don't need a man to earn for me, to put a roof over my head, to make day-to-day decisions for me. I gave off the impression that I was completely self-sufficient. But being self-sufficient doesn't mean that I don't need someone. I wanted someone to love me. I wanted someone to need me. Evidently, I gave the impression that I was a superwoman and could do it all alone. Hearing this made me realize I needed to work on what impression I was giving. How could I make myself vulnerable enough to demonstrate my need for love without giving up the strength I was unwilling to compromise?

The shrew made every man in the kingdom feel as if they didn't have a chance with her because of the overwhelming personality trait she demonstrated. No one thought they could get anywhere near her, let alone her heart. One man took a shot. He took a chance. He confronted her anger and told her he wasn't responsible for the anger she seemed to feel toward everyone.

ON JANUARY 12, 2012, JOSHUA BELL, A WORLD-RENOWNED CONCERT VIOLINIST, DRESSED IN DIRTY JEANS, A T-SHIRT, AND BALL CAP, LAY HIS VIOLIN CASE AT HIS FEET, AND PLAYED. SECURITY VIDEO SHOWS HIM STANDING IN A WASHINGTON, DC, METRO STATION, GIVING A BRIEF CONCERT MOST PEOPLE IGNORE. SOME TOSS MONEY INTO THE CASE AND MOVE ON, TOO BUSY TO NOTICE THE STUNNING BEAUTY OF HIS PLAYING. ONE WOMAN FINALLY STOPS, A LONE FIGURE STANDING STILL AS EVERYONE ELSE RUSHES AROUND HER. A FEW OTHERS JOIN HER TO STAND AND WATCH. WHEN BELL FINISHES, THE WOMAN REVEALS SHE RECOGNIZED HIM AS THE FAMOUS VIRTUOSO.[60]

THE PERSON YOU ARE TRYING TO CONNECT WITH IS
NOT THE ONE RESPONSIBLE FOR YOUR PAIN.

Don't try to make them pay for what someone or something else has done. In your search, you will find there are people who might be willing to entertain that pain for a short while, but in the end, they won't tolerate anger directed at them that they did not earn. Why should they? They want to love you. The problem may be you aren't ready to love yourself and, therefore, aren't ready for anyone else to love you. You have to love yourself enough to heal so that you can be found among the rubble.

If there's nothing else you get from this chapter, hear this: if you allow the pain of your past to cripple your future, your future won't look so bright.

WHAT ARE YOUR FLAWS?

We've talked about understanding your value (Chapter 2), but we all have flaws. What are yours? Discuss what you think are your flaws with your friends and family. Would you consider that you may need therapy to overcome some of your flaws?

Examples:
- You have difficulty trusting new partners.
- You don't feel comfortable sharing your feelings.
- You self-sabotage.

HOW HAVE YOU BEEN HURT?

When mistakes are made, it's always a good idea to look at what happened and what you could/should have done differently. We're going to get through this quickly and not wallow in the bad stuff. So here's the assignment: think of your past relationships and what hurt you. List the hurts.

Examples:
- You were never introduced to your partner's family and friends.
- You needed them and they weren't there.
- You felt you made compromises but didn't get them in return.

COMMON DENOMINATOR

Now that you have your list, is there a common denominator? In the person you were with? In the way the relationship ended? If there was something you could have done differently for each one, that might be the common denominator you are looking for.

CHAPTER TWENTY-TWO
My Bad Batch

The only real stumbling block is fear of failure.
In cooking you've got to have a what-the-hell attitude.
—Julia Child [61]

Telling personal stories isn't my favorite thing to do. Making mistakes and then admitting them to the world is not fun, but I will do it for you. We're going to talk about counterfeits in the next chapter, but before we do that, I want to tell you about my run-in with a bad batch.

Have you ever made cookies? Whether you made them from scratch, from a mix in a box, or used the premade dough where all you have to do is cut them up and put them on a cookie sheet, there's always the chance that you'll make a mistake. Maybe you pulled them from the oven too late, and they're all scorched on the bottom. Maybe you set the temperature too high, and they came out brown on the outside but raw on the inside. For whatever reason, you find that you have a bad batch of cookies. They are inedible. You can't save them.

If you bake, you're probably going to burn a few cookies.

BURNING COOKIES, MAKING A MISTAKE IN YOUR BAKING, OR NOT
GETTING THE RECIPE RIGHT CAN ALL BE EMBARRASSING. BUT YOU
TOSS OUT THE BURNT ONES, AND YOU START ALL OVER AGAIN.

There may be some of you reading this book who are starting all over again. If you're searching through the rubble or digging through the haystack, you may run into a bad batch. It can be painful. It can be very hard. But some batches are bad for you, and you'll have to make the decision to throw them out.

There's also the possibility that you were someone else's bad batch. Perhaps you have to start over because you were rejected for whatever reason.

No matter the scenario that has you starting over again, you are back to searching through the rubble, digging in the haystack. You may want to push thoughts of your bad batch out of your mind. You don't want to think about those scorched cookies. If you're going to learn from your mistakes, like any good baker would, sometimes you need to take a look at where you went wrong. You may not ever be able to completely avoid making a bad batch or being someone else's bad batch, but you can make sure they are less likely to happen.

Rejection is a hard thing to overcome. You feel like those cookies that get tossed in the trash—unsalvageable, unwanted. Unfortunately, if you're searching through the haystack, rejection is almost inevitable. I never promised this would be easy. I hope these pages will at least help you prepare for it.

I'm going to tell you a story I've never told anyone. You're getting it firsthand because I've decided to put it in the pages of this book.

I dated a young man for about a year. For the sake of storytelling, let's call him Burny. (Get it? Burnt cookies? Burny?) So Burny and I had spent a great deal of time together in that year. We'd been to concerts together, enjoyed many late-night conversations, celebrated birthdays, and had romantic dinners. He'd met my children. We were in a loving, committed relationship. He told me he loved me. I told him I loved him.

Burny enjoyed cooking, and one morning, he made my lunch for me to take to work. It was a surprise. The gesture touched me. I went to work happy and filled with emotion. I spent my morning at work, in a New York public school at that time, looking forward to eating the chicken salad sandwich that had been made by Burny, a man I loved, a man who claimed he loved me too.

I sat down with some friends to have my lunch. We were talking, discussing the day, when my speech became slurred. I could feel my face and body begin to slouch. Thankfully, my friends noticed. One of them said, "Call 911. Jameliah is having a stroke!"

I thank God that my friends had been there and knew exactly what was happening. As I'm writing this today, I know that without their quick action, I may not have ever fully recovered.

As I was strapped to the gurney and loaded into the ambulance, I thought about how I wasn't going to be able to enjoy that sandwich because I was having a stroke. I also thought about my children and what my life might be like afterward. I was having a stroke. Would I survive this? Would I lose some of my capabilities? I was petrified.

I arrived at the hospital, and even though I was having a stroke, I was well aware of all that was going on around me. I knew my children were safe because they were with their father. My coworkers were there, and I knew they had notified my family, who had then notified Burny. We'd been involved for a year at that time, and they knew who he was. Of course, they had let him know what was going on.

A few hours later, after treatments, I became more lucid. I looked at my phone and scrolled through calls and messages from well-wishers. There wasn't a call or text or anything from Burny.

I lay in my hospital bed, frightened for my future, praying for a full recovery. The hours and the days went by, and the man who claimed he loved me was nowhere in sight. I'd had a stroke! I was going through the most difficult period of my life, and the man I thought might be a good match for me wasn't there. No text message, no phone call, no flowers, no card.

Absolute silence.

After about a week, I asked my sister to get in touch with him. Maybe something had happened to him. There had to be an explanation for why he wasn't by my side. My sister told me that he'd said he loved me but that he "got caught up."

What did that mean?

More weeks went by. Recovering from a stroke, even a mild one like I had, is long and hard and lonely. It took months. Still, I never heard from Burny. Not even once.

After a few months, I tried calling him. I left messages for him. I sent him emails. He never responded. Finally, I decided I needed to know what had happened, so I confronted him.

He told me he'd been in a difficult place. He said he didn't know how much I would recover, and he didn't want the responsibility of caring for someone who was impaired. It was difficult to hear, but he told me his truth. It hurt that he didn't have the courage to tell me at the time and waited to be confronted before opening up about it.

ACCORDING TO A 2009 ARTICLE IN SCIENCE DAILY, MEN ARE SIX TIMES MORE LIKELY TO SEPARATE OR DIVORCE THEIR PARTNER SOON AFTER THE PARTNER IS DIAGNOSED WITH A SERIOUS ILLNESS LIKE MULTIPLE SCLEROSIS OR CANCER. THE RATE OF DIVORCE WHEN THE MALE IS SICK WAS 2.9 PERCENT, COMPARED TO THAT OF WHEN THE WOMAN IS SICK AT 20.8 PERCENT. THE LONGER THE RELATIONSHIP OR MARRIAGE LASTED, THE BETTER CHANCE IT WOULD SURVIVE THE ILLNESS.[62]

He had to know that his absence was painful at a time when I needed him most. Instead of being honest about his misgivings, he simply ghosted me.

I share this story with you for total transparency. We're talking here about finding a needle in a haystack. We're talking about the hope and promise of love and partnership. We're talking about searching through the rubble and sifting through the possibilities. To talk about these things, we also have to talk about the potential for landing on a bad batch.

Your bad batch may not be easily identified. Those cookies may smell nice. They might look nice and brown and golden. It's not until you bite into them that you find out you used salt when the recipe called for sugar. That cookie needs to go directly into the trash.

On your search, you're going to roll up on people who look the part, smell the part, sound the part. They may seem like the perfect sweet to stick in your lunch box or save for your evening snack. They may seem like the great, big, chocolate dessert you've been craving.

If they end up being a bad batch, toss them out. Don't spend any more time on them. That sweet may have looked like the real thing, but it lacked the ingredients for the true substance you need. You are going to find batches that do not qualify.

When I look at my life now, I can finally say with assurance that Burny didn't qualify. I trusted in God. I kept that trust as I searched through the rubble until someone found me. Like me, you will be in the right place at the right time when your fit will find you.

Each batch you go through is supposed to be different. There may be subtle differences, or the differences can be like night and day. The main thing to remember is that if you find a bad batch, toss it out and move on.

Most people don't know I've had more than one stroke. Even if Burny had acted the way a man in a loving relationship was supposed to act, he may have ghosted me during the second event. No, he didn't treat me right. But if he had, would I be here in the amazing marriage I am in now? I ran into a bad batch, but now I can say without a shadow of a doubt that I have found my fit for a lifetime.

Think about the people who didn't treat you properly. Think about the people who rejected you. Think about writing them a thank-you letter! And then make a list of them and include what it was about them that landed them in the bad-batch category.

Keep reading. We have more work to do. And make a list of everyone who rejected you. In the next chapter, we'll look more at bad batches—or counterfeits—and how you can make them easier to identify.

WRITE A LETTER

Was there a relationship in your past that ended in a way that felt unfinished or was hurtful or damaging to you? Take a minute to consider writing a letter to the person who hurt you. Identify what it was they did that caused you pain.

CHAPTER TWENTY-THREE
The Opposite of Real

counterfeit (ˈkaūn-tər-fit) *adjective,* made in imitation of
something else with intent to deceive; insincere, feigned; imitation[63]

In the next chapter, we're going to talk about The Real Thing (TRT). We all want to know how to identify it. Finding TRT is what this book is all about, right?

What we do know is that, along the search path, you're probably going to have at least one instance when, instead of finding true love, you find a counterfeit. You're digging through the hay or scrambling through the rubble, and you come up with something you think is your needle. It sure looks like the real thing. It may even feel like the real thing. You might think you ran up on something that was so authentically pure, you're convinced this has to be it.

Eureka, right?

Not quite. How can we know? By what standard can we judge whether this person who has captured your attention, perhaps even captured your heart, is the right one for you?

Remember what Miki Howard said in the song "Love Under New Management"? She says experience is the best teacher. Experience teaches you what games people play in their pursuit of love.

So to avoid the counterfeit, we're going to take a moment to study it. Through study of what has happened before, you can let experience be your teacher so you can fully understand what it is you *don't* want.

Let me tell you what I did to help my journey. I sat down and identified all the counterfeits I had encountered throughout the years. I fully identified them—what happened, why they were counterfeit, and what I knew I didn't want to ever encounter again. By the time I pricked my finger on my needle, by the time my journey had finally ended by finding my husband, true love could not have gotten away if it had tried! Everything about my husband felt different, looked different, and sounded different. My real thing asked me, "What can I do for you?" Instead of, "What can you do for me?" My real thing's children said, "Let us love you," instead of someone saying, "Do for me and *my* children."

Counterfeits, as painful and scary as they may be, teach us lessons. Sometimes the pain of a failed relationship makes you want to just forget about it. To file it away somewhere and never look at it again. But you should look at it. You need to look at it. If you need to have a therapist help you look at it, do that, but don't throw away the lessons your past has taught you because you're too afraid to revisit them.

It might have been loneliness that drove us to our counterfeits or desperation that sparked the desire to make some wrong decisions. We've already talked about this. Instead of beating yourself up about it, examine it, understand it, and learn from it.

When I wrote my last book, I had been duped by a counterfeit. Most of us have at one time or another. The counterfeit is almost like the devil, for those of you who have faith. The counterfeit comes to injure, to steal, and to destroy, whereas the real thing comes to build up, to bring value, and to heal.

Are you a part of my Car Chronicles Movement? The Car Chronicles refers to the Facebook live conversations I have every day, and I mean, every single day—Monday through Sunday— whether I'm traveling, on vacation, or working my butt off like I normally do. I will always find time at 7:30 a.m. to go live on

Facebook to speak to you. Thousands of people tune in every day. It is a loving commitment I make. It's not easy, but I'm gonna keep at it as long as there are people who want to keep listening.

Anyway, during the Car Chronicles, I always say you gotta watch the fruit. It's easy to avoid the red flags, to forget about your list, to stumble into something that is fruit-less. We will talk about the fruit in the next chapter. For now, let's all agree that it's easy—all too easy—to be fooled by the counterfeit.

When I sat down and examined my past relationships and identified the counterfeits, it was so much easier to identify the kinds of things they had in common. It's so easy to think that a relationship ended because the other person was bad, or there was one event or thing that made you walk away. Then, once you've identified that thing, you don't examine it any further.

Now that you're meeting people, you need to be able to put a name to the attributes that led past relationships in the wrong direction. If you're dating someone who has attributes that match counterfeits of the past, I'm gonna need you to pump your brakes. Give it some time. Let the layers of the onion peel away, and hopefully, it won't take long for the counterfeit to reveal themself.

I've found that for me, a common theme for a counterfeit has been that they are users. Soon, they won't be able to help themselves from attempting to suck you dry.

This all may sound a little harsh. I'm gonna bet, whether you're a man or a woman, you will recognize some of this.

How to identify a counterfeit.

A counterfeit:

- insists you are crazy for questioning them;
- insists you are confused about what did or didn't happen;
- pleads innocence;
- says they had good intentions that went wrong;
- will fully demonstrate their jealousy;
- has an incessant need for discord;
- is hungry for your constant attention;
- has motives that aren't always clear;

- will be fast and loose with the truth and may enlist you to assist in their lies to other people;
- will constantly ask to do what works for them and ignore the things you need;
- will try to hide how broken they are;
- will break you too.

When you've identified two or more of these behaviors, it might be time to cut that counterfeit loose.

The worst part about the counterfeit is that you may be in one of those relationships now, but because of the manipulation, the counterfeit has made you afraid to leave.

THE COUNTERFEIT MAY MAKE YOU THINK YOU WILL
NEVER FIND SOMEONE TO LOVE YOU THE WAY YOU DESERVE.
THE COUNTERFEIT MAY HAVE LEFT YOU SO HURT THAT
YOU'VE DECIDED NEVER TO LOOK FOR LOVE AGAIN.

The thing about counterfeits is, they can look a lot like the real thing. They can be long and sharp and silver, just like the needle you want, but they don't stand up under the pressure.

Needles are strong. Needles are hard to break. The same is true of real love because it is unbreakable. Love knows endurance, and love knows how to overcome adversity. Keep on searching with your eyes open and your heart ready to receive, and love will find you. It will sting, but that search through the haystack you are wading through will be worth it. The process you go through will lead you to a place where the pain feels very different.

CHAPTER TWENTY-FOUR
How Do U Know It's TRT?

There ain't nothing like the real thing, baby.
There ain't nothing like the real thing.
—Lyrics by Nicholas Ashford and
Valerie Simpson, 1968[64]

Would you go panning for gold if you didn't know what gold looked like? You could be out there doing backbreaking work, investing a lifetime of money and energy, searching for something you can't identify, even if it's right in front of you. Finding your fit is one of the most difficult things to do, but part of that difficulty is not knowing what you're looking for.

In the previous chapter, we talked about counterfeits, and I'm convinced that the ability to identify a counterfeit is helpful in understanding what you need to avoid when searching for your fit.

Trust me: when you finally understand what it is you're searching for, it will feel like finding the solution to a mystery.

This is the point we've wanted to reach when we started this journey. You've written your list. You're ready to date in a way that helps you gather data and explore the person sitting across from you. You're ready to listen to family and friends about the people who may be right for you. Maybe you're ready to enlist a matchmaker. Maybe you're ready to give some people who are already in your world a second look. Most importantly, maybe you're ready to do some soul-searching, self-discovery, and healing from experiences of the past that may be obstacles to finding true happiness today. You've looked at past mistakes, identified the counterfeits, and can readily identify them now. At the very least, maybe you've come to grips with the way past heartache can impact your current search, and once you're aware of the impacts, you can work around them.

And now here we are. Imagining what we may find at the end of our search. I feel a song in my spirit as we talk about our search for the perfect needle, and we think about what is waiting for us at the end of that search. We are searching through the haystack, digging through the rubble. We are looking for a needle. But here is the key.

How do we know it's the right needle for us?

A song comes to mind. Ashford and Simpson wrote about it. A whole bunch of people sang about it such as Marvin Gaye, Tammi Terrell, and Aretha Franklin. Even Boyz II Men offered their own rendition.

"There ain't nothing like The Real Thing."

As I've said, you may find a whole lot of things are sharp, long, silver, and look like a needle. But don't be fooled. They may not be your needle. You may have run across a bad batch. Maybe you've run across a counterfeit. Understanding both of those things will help you obtain your goal.

And the goal is to find The Real Thing. When you actually find TRT, you will have this authentic experience of finding something special. It's almost like you are finding something so special, no one else on the planet has made this discovery. It's an amazing feeling. But don't let that feeling overwhelm everything you've learned. You want authenticity. You want longevity. You want to make sure it's TRT.

Imagine the *Jeopardy* music playing in the background. The host starts the game. The contestant says, "Romance for $1 million." The square turns, and the host reads the clue. "True love," he says.

The contestant responds in the form of a question with, "How do know you've found it?"

The host says, "That is correct!"

How do know you found it? That's the million-dollar question. Let's face it. The Real Thing can be a bit frightening to admit. But if you're looking for TRT, how do you *know* it's TRT?

The answer is to watch for the fruit.

The *fruit*, you say? Now, you really think I'm crazy.

Since we married, my husband and I have taught a series of seminars about relationships. Our Coupling talks are aimed at helping people identify the pitfalls of their partnership before they become problems. We hope to offer new ways of understanding familiar patterns of behavior, ways to find the goodness in each other and to keep the love alive. When your eyes and hearts are open to them, you can also identify the fruits of your love.

I also teach a class called Watch the Fruit. It's a class based on biblical teachings, but trust me, no matter what religion you may or may not practice, I think this will be very helpful for you. Give me your attention for a few minutes, and you'll see what I mean.

When we're talking about fruit, we're talking about the fruits of the spirit as they are written about in Galatians 5:16–23. It's a rather long passage, so I won't quote it here. Look for the full section at the end of this chapter. You don't have to go read it right now, but it may help you pull some pieces together later. For now, know that there are nine fruits of the spirit, and they are spelled out as clear as day in Galatians 5:16–23.

Now watch this. I see these fruits of the spirit as all the ingredients, every single last morsel you need to create this fruit salad we can call TRT. No one walks around with these fruits painted on their skin. You have to watch for them; you have to dig for them. One person might make a particular fruit of yours shrivel and die. Another person could cause that same fruit to ripen to its fullest because it is love that motivates the fruit to flourish.

Hang in here with me. This is important stuff, and a nugget in this book that you don't want to miss. It will all make sense in just a minute.

One of the nine fruits is love, of course. Love is the fruit that will not only help you identify these other fruits in others, but it will also help others see the fruits in you.

WHEN LOVE IS IN ABUNDANCE, IT BECOMES A LENS THROUGH WHICH YOU CAN SEE THESE ATTRIBUTES IN OTHERS AND THE LENS THAT WILL HELP OTHERS SEE THOSE SAME ATTRIBUTES IN YOU.

But there are all kinds of love, right? There's sibling love. There's the kind of love you have for your pets, the kind of love you have for your favorite hobbies, even the kind of love you have for your favorite dessert. I love strawberry shortcake. I don't love strawberry shortcake the same way I love my husband.

The love you have for TRT, and the love your TRT has for you is completely different than all others. That basic love emotion will unleash these other fruits in both of you, so they become active and visible to both of you. Without that basic love, some of these fruits may remain invisible or unknown to you.

What are the other fruits?

ALONG WITH LOVE, THE FRUITS ARE JOY, PEACE, FORBEARANCE, KINDNESS, GOODNESS, FAITHFULNESS, AND SELF CONTROL.

What does any of that mean?

Imagine someone tells you they love you. They say they are crazy about you. They spend night after night, week after week, telling you that you are the one and only for them. Eventually, in time, you learn that their love only extends up to the point where your pain begins to cause them a problem.

Remember my story about having a stroke? I was dating Burny and spending the majority of my days and nights in a life built around this man. We had declared our love for each other. But

Burny's love could not withstand the test of my illness. When I felt pain, he couldn't support me in my trouble.

Love is consistent. The person who loves you has forbearance or patience for your troubles, just as your love will have forbearance for theirs. Burny's love wasn't enough to fertilize one of the most basic of the nine fruits—patience. You see what I mean?

If you've spent any time looking for your needle, I can almost guarantee that you've experienced pain in some way. I'm not talking about physical pain such as with my stroke. I'm talking about extreme heartache, the crushing pain of disappointment, the pain of losing a job or a loved one, the pain of a newly remembered trauma in your past.

Pain is one of those things that can reveal TRT most emphatically. If you are feeling pain, if you have tears, TRT will want to ease you of that pain.

Not all pain is controllable, but deliberate pain should never be part of the problem. He or she is going to do everything in their power to ensure you're not hurt and to ease you of your pain. At the very least, they will carry the pain with you. If it's within their power, he or she will change the behavior that caused the pain in the first place. Their goodness, their willingness to be concerned about you, is one of the nine fruits.

Now, there are times when it's impossible to prevent someone from feeling pain. Sometimes, a blending of the fruits is necessary.

Imagine you are in love with a medical doctor, and that doctor is called away for an emergency during a birthday celebration you've been planning for weeks. It can't be helped. They've got to go because it's their duty. Their departure may cause you pain, but they wanted to be at the party. Their goodness and faithfulness drive them to perform their duty, and it's those fruits that made you love them in the first place. You know from their actions and words that if they could prevent your pain in that moment, they would. In return, your love gives you the forbearance to extend the understanding they need to do the work they've been called to do. The fruits of goodness, faithfulness, and forbearance are alive and well in this relationship.

In biblical teachings, God calls these attributes "the fruits of the spirit." They are characteristics that will become visible to you over time. Some may show themselves early and remain consistent. Others could take weeks or months, require tests and tribulations to see. The time it takes for your awareness of these fruits to become clear is a very good reason why sleeping with someone on the first date is not a good idea. Lust, of course, can cloud your ability to see these attributes clearly.

What is amazing about these fruits is that while you are watching for them in your potential fit, you will, at the same time, begin to recognize how the fruits manifest themselves within yourself. Does this person draw the goodness, kindness, and peace out of you? The Real Thing will make you discover these fruits inside you because you and your partner's love will allow these characteristics to be seen.

THE REAL THING WILL MAKE YOU DISCOVER THESE FRUITS INSIDE
YOU BECAUSE YOUR LOVE WILL ALLOW THEM TO BE SEEN.

The Real Thing practices kindness and goodness in difficult situations.

The Real Thing is not afraid of your problems or the things that keep you up at night. They are ready to help you with them just as you are ready to help them with theirs. In fact, TRT says to "bring it on" because one of the most important attributes is patience— or forbearance.

The Real Thing is faithful. To be faithful doesn't just cover not tipping out on someone. Faithfulness is fidelity. Faithfulness is being true to someone, meaning your relationship is not based on lies. The Real Thing is faithful, which also makes them consistent. You are ready to stand beside each other. You can trust in the constancy of TRT. Faithfulness means you don't have to worry that they will be by your side when needed.

Here's one I'd like you to take a minute to consider. The Real Thing is not afraid. The Bible says, "There is no fear in love, but perfect love casts out fear. For fear has to do with punishment, and whoever fears has not been perfected in love" (1 John 4:18, ESV).[65]

Bottom line, when you roll up on TRT, you're not afraid to love them, and you're not afraid to receive the love.

The Real Thing understands there is a risk to being with you. You are both taking the risk that you could be hurt; TRT is willing to accept that risk because you are a ruby, and you are worth it!

The Real Thing is not afraid of whatever life has dealt you because they are ready to help make things better, not worse, just as you are ready to do the same with them. The Real Thing is a partner, willing to help you carry the weight of life.

The Real Thing is not afraid of your past, and you are not afraid of theirs because, together, you know you can help build a better future. The Real Thing brings you both a level of peace that says instead of fighting each other, you will band together to take on the world.

This may be the most important part about watching the fruit. To find your fit, to find TRT, you cannot rush things. You would never expect to step into an orchard and find all these fruits of the spirit at the same time. Neither should you expect to meet someone and see all these fruits at the first hello. You've got to peel back layers and they need to peel back your layers, because you're both looking for the fruits in each other.

Over time, you may learn that a fruit such as goodness from him may bring out another fruit such as forbearance from you. You may get your fruit of joy from cooking a lavish, delicious meal. Your ability to cook may bring out the fruit of kindness and self-control to be revealed in him because he can enjoy the meal but won't expect you to serve him every night. What fruits are revealed in him as he interacts with your parents? What fruits are revealed in you as that meeting is going on? What fruits are revealed when she attends your office function? What fruits does she find while you interact with her around your colleagues?

The Real Thing isn't going to ostracize you from your family for their sake; TRT realizes that when they make you a part of their life, your family is part of what you are building together, for better or worse.

Two people may not be on the same page on everything. When two people who love each other disagree, they know that disagreement can impact what they are trying to build together. So use conflict resolution, which is based on the fruits both people demonstrate. Their disagreements are resolved through patience, kindness, self-control, and love.

I've told you before, repetition is the mother of learning, so I'm going to keep telling you what TRT really is.

Does your potential real fit come into the relationship understanding that you may not know what love is? In that situation, TRT will have the forbearance, goodness, kindness, and faithfulness to work through that issue so you can see and feel what true love is. Do you have the selflessness to teach someone else how to love? You won't know the answer to that question until you meet someone and have enough love in your heart to bring that other fruit forward.

An appropriate verse is, "If the iron is blunt, and one does not sharpen the edge, he must use more strength, but wisdom helps one to succeed" (Ecclesiastes 10:10, ESV).[66]

What that scripture says to me is, if you roll up on TRT, and they lack one of the fruits, your own fruits of love and forbearance should be ready to help them sharpen what they have that is dull. Yes, your love can help them do that. Isn't that amazing?

The Real Thing is consistent; it gives, it sacrifices, it does not lie, it doesn't have an ulterior motive, it comes to fix what has been damaged. The Real Thing asks the question, "How do *we* fix it?"

Finding TRT is so amazing. Let me tell you what TRT can do.

A COUNTERFEIT CAN LEAVE YOU FOR DEAD, BUT THE REAL THING CAN RESUSCITATE THAT HEART AND MAKE IT READY FOR LOVE.

Here is the full passage in Galatians that outlines the fruits of love. I hope you will take some extra time to consider this passage and this chapter. Think about what all this means to you and your search. Discuss it and take the time to consider the final exercise in the workbook.

> (16) I say this to you: Let the Holy Spirit lead you in each step. Then you will not please your sinful old selves. (17) The things our old selves want to do are against what the Holy Spirit wants. The Holy Spirit does not agree with what our sinful old selves want. These two are against each other. So you cannot do what you want to do. (18) If you let the Holy Spirit lead you, the Law no longer has power over you. (19) The things your sinful old self wants to do are: sex sins, sinful desires, wild living, (20) worshiping false gods, witchcraft, hating, fighting, being jealous, being angry, arguing, dividing into little groups and thinking the other groups are wrong, false teaching, (21) wanting something someone else has, killing other people, using strong drink, wild parties, and all things like these. I told you before and I am telling you again that those who do these things will have no place in the holy nation of God. (22) But the Holy Spirit produces this kind of fruit in our lives: love, joy, peace, patience, kindness, goodness, faithfulness, (23) gentleness, and self-control. There is no law against these things! (Galatians 5:16–23, ESV).[67]

FRUITS OF LOVE

Now that you know about the nine fruits of love (**love, joy, peace, patience, kindness, goodness, faithfulness, gentleness, and self-control**), take another look at your list. Do the characteristics on your list reflect any of the fruits? Are there additions you can make to your list to incorporate the nine fruits of love?

CHAPTER TWENTY-FIVE
My Bloody Valentine

From all the questions I get about it, I know there is an interest in hearing how I met my husband and what the story is behind our relationship. In this chapter, I'm going to tell you about it. Stick with me while I set it up for you.

For those of you who are single and waiting, we've already talked about some of the land mines you may run across. There are many days when it's just downright uncomfortable to not have a mate. From weddings to events where you're supposed to bring a plus-one to New Year's Eve to family gatherings where your dating life is the topic of conversation and gossip. It's hard out there for a single person! And for single people, there may not be a more uncomfortable day than Valentine's Day. The stores are full of red hearts and boxes of candy, flowers, and row upon row of cards to help someone proclaim their love. Seriously. It can be downright annoying.

This year, Valentine's Day rolled around while I was working on this book, and I couldn't help but think about all the people who are digging through that haystack for their needle. I know how hard it is! Believe me.

Some people look upon February 14 with disfavor because of its pagan festival history, and indeed, there are many who believe the holiday started that way. Others call it a quasi holiday built on the capitalistic need to sell stuff. If you're single and waiting, pagan or capitalist, you probably anticipate it with a sense of dread. I don't blame you.

On the other hand, there are some who look forward to the holiday, planning it out, investing wholeheartedly in that one day of the year when love is lionized. I've learned my husband is one of these. I'm going to remember 2021 as the best Valentine's Day of my life. My husband obviously wanted to do something extra special for me, and he succeeded in every measure. He made Valentine's Day the most amazing day I have ever experienced. And it wasn't so much about where he took me or what he gave me or how big the surprise was or any of that. It was the most amazing day because it was truly a day of love.

While writing this book, having that kind of Valentine's Day made me think about so many who are searching desperately through that haystack. So many are looking for that special someone who gives them butterflies and makes their heart race.

On the other hand, Valentine's Day and New Year's Eve and all those other days and events that make you feel so alone are absolutely the worst times for you to feel desperate for that special someone. February 1 is the undeniably wrong time to be searching through the rubble for a Valentine's Day date. The office Christmas party is the wrong time to be looking for a New Year's Eve party date. Despite what might happen on the Hallmark Channel, the weekend before your college reunion is the wrong time to be begging someone to come with you to pretend they are your long-time relationship.

But at this point in the book, I don't need to tell you all that. You know it.

AS YOU'RE WORKING YOUR WAY THROUGH THESE CHAPTERS, YOU'VE ALREADY LEARNED THAT THE BEST TIME—REALLY, THE ONLY TIME—TO FIND SOMEONE IS WHEN YOU'RE NOT LOOKING.

Plenty of us have made wrong decisions and invested our hearts in someone or some relationship that not only wasn't worthy of our love but also left us crushed. We know that pain is associated with love. It just is. But there is good pain and bad pain.

There's pain that comes from loving someone so much, time away from them hurts. There's the pain of loving someone so much that their pain is your pain. That's a good kind of pain.

If you've ever born a child, you know that once you get past the shoulders, which is the hardest and most painful part, that agony goes away because of the reward. That's another one of the good kinds of pain.

February 14, Valentine's Day, can be felt in one extreme or another. Some will find true pleasure in it, the way I did with my husband this year. For others, the day can be more like a bloody valentine, and that is not worth it.

What do I mean by a bloody valentine?

A bloody valentine is when you go digging in the rubble you rejected in the past. You think retreading some old territory might be a good idea because you've convinced yourself you're not going to spend another Valentine's Day alone. Or maybe you go searching for some piece of rubble you knew wasn't right for you when you set it aside before, but suddenly, on February 10, it starts to look pretty good. You know neither of those scenarios is going to end well, but you do it anyway.

I know firsthand what a bloody valentine is like. I tried to retread old ground. I tried to breathe new life into something I should have left for dead. I remember standing in the shower after having gone through one of the most horrific experiences in my life. I wrote about it in my previous book. If I told you the details of how I had been manipulated, used, and abused, you wouldn't believe it. If I retold all of the heartache and the hell I went through, you would tell me I'm exaggerating. I'm not.

The year I had my bloody Valentine's Day, the year that left me crying and bereft, I thought I would never, ever find the love I craved. Loneliness and heartache left me feeling as low as I'd ever been. As I cried and castigated myself, I came to the conclusion that my search was over. I'd done the work on myself, I'd searched through every straw of hay in my haystack, and my needle simply was not there. I was done.

Like so many of you, I was tired of looking, tired of failing. Finally, I prayed and asked God for help. Now this is my truth, so allow me to tell you that I asked God for something specific. Don't let the mention of God and all that he has done for me turn you away from my truth. If you give someone the opportunity to share their truth, it may set your thought process free to hear and allow you to feel things you otherwise might not have. So my truth is, I was crying and distraught, and I asked God for what I needed and wanted, and he gave it to me in abundance. He gave me more than I could have ever imagined.

I told you a bit about this in previous chapters. Before I met him, my husband, the man who just gave me the most memorable Valentine's Day of my life, had performed the marriage ceremony for my older sister and her husband. My sister and I are close, but I wasn't able to attend her wedding because I was out of the country attending a conference. I'd never met her pastor. Over many years, she'd had a long and very close relationship with this man I knew little about. He'd even had many conversations with my dad, who has now passed, that I wasn't privy to. My sister had her friends, and I had mine. My husband was in my sister's life but not yet in mine.

Several days after my bloody Valentine's Day, my sister called me. She told me about a friend of hers who was freshly single. "I believe he would be a good match for you," she said. "You know him. He's my pastor."

Now I have to say that for reasons of my own, I knew, without doubt, without question, that I didn't want to be involved with a pastor! *Nope.* No way. Not happening. I'm not saying pastors make bad lovers. I'm only saying that I never thought a two-pastor relationship would work.

But after hearing this from my sister, something gave me peace. Just a few days before, I'd had the worst Valentine's Day ever and was the saddest and loneliest I'd ever been. The timing gave me pause. I had to give her suggestion some thought.

I don't have to tell you if you're reading this book—you know that pickin's ain't easy. I know you agree because you're sifting through that haystack right now. Yes, it's hard, but let's take a minute to talk about hope.

My sister and I had this long conversation about the gentleman she thought was right for me. She reminded me several times that I knew him already. "He's been my friend for years," she said. To be honest, when she'd spoken of him before, I'd been too busy running around the world to conferences and lectures and doing what I had to do to pay too much attention to the people in my sister's life. So while she kept insisting that I surely must know him, I didn't really. She wasn't giving up. She said, "I want you to go and just check him out. Take a look at him."

I told her I'd looked at his social media accounts years before. I knew what he looked like. I knew what she'd told me about him, but I didn't understand why she seemed so sure, so insistent that I should take a closer look.

Finally, she said, "There is something I know about the both of you. I know that you won't hurt each other."

Now remember, just over a week previously, I'd been so hurt and dejected. I'd just climbed out of the shower crying my head off over my hurt and heartache. I knew, intimately, what that kind of pain felt like. The last thing in the world I wanted at that point was to ever feel it again. And my sister was telling me that even if it didn't work, at least it wouldn't hurt.

"Okay. Okay," I said.

When I did finally meet my future husband—this time, with the backing of our mutual matchmaker, my sister—I saw something in his eyes, in his smile. What I saw was something familiar. I saw pain. I saw heart-wrenching pain. The same kind of pain I had just felt. The same kind of pain that had me crumpled in the shower. It was pain that I wanted to heal.

When you're searching for your needle, you often search for something familiar. That can work for you but can also work against you. This time, that familiarity in his gaze said to me, "I was there too."

It was as if we'd been searching through the haystack and ended up in the exact same place at the exact same time. In his gaze, I saw that he'd found something valuable in me that others had overlooked or mistreated.

We had our first phone conversation, and that conversation has continued since then. While we'd had a disastrous first date, as I said previously, our connection from the start was real and the reason why a bad first date wasn't the end of the fulfilling relationship we have now.

He'd been in the periphery of my life for years. He recounted stories and conversations he'd had with my dad, words I otherwise would never have heard. He'd been there the entire time.

He was the needle that was right under my nose!

There may be a needle under your nose as well. It may not reveal itself until the right moment or until you are in the right space to see it.

To stretch this metaphor a bit more, I've said before the point of the needle is sharp. I often think of that first realization—when you've found your fit—as the prick of the needle. That prick is the way that needle grasps your attention and lets you know it's there.

For me, the end of the needle was pain and heartache. When I met my husband and felt that initial prick, I looked at him and realized I wanted to show him something he'd never seen before. I wanted to show him me. The real me. I wanted to be the thread in his needle that pulls and connects the woven pieces of our lives together to make a warm quilt. A quilt that will comfort him in a cold world.

This is gonna sound crazy, but I heard the "The Star-Spangled Banner," with the flutes and drums and rockets flaring—and there may have been lightning too. There was this undeniable comfort that the pain in my past would no longer be part of my future. My bloody valentine heart—the one that had me curled up and sobbing, feeling broken and bereft—healed itself.

I'm telling you all this to give you some hope. Hope that the pain you've accumulated in your search was not for nothing. The experiences you've gone through and the struggles you've had may help connect you with someone who has had similar experiences. It's all part of who you are.

I believe that timing is everything. If I'd met my husband earlier, if I hadn't had the life experiences I'd had, the connection may not have been made. At any other time, I may not have had the wisdom to see the pain I saw so clearly in his eyes. My gratitude is in the timing and my connection with him.

I know how hard you are looking for what I found. I understand it. The search is never easy, but my wish is that you will find hope within these pages and that the words here will help you find what you are looking for. My wish is that one day, that bloody, damaged heart of yours will stop beating in discomfort and start beating with the adrenaline of love. That heart of yours that shattered, the one that made you feel broken and ready to quit can heal, and it can love again. As we reach the end of this book, you know that there is work you need to do. My wish is that these pages have helped you see what you need to do, what you need to fix within yourself.

You owe it to yourself to love again, live again, and heal. Let this search open your world and lead you to experience new things. Let new people heal the holes in your heart. Find joy in stepping out in ways you've not tried before. Work toward being a person who is not only ready to find someone worthy of you but someone who is worthy of being found.

When you do finally find your perfect fit, when you finally find that needle that is everything you hoped it would be, wouldn't it be nice if, later, when your relationship has matured and you're reminiscing about what it was like to find each other, you, together, can think of your search fondly? Both of you went on that search, and you both had your frustrations, but at the same time, there is an incredible pleasure in it.

Share what you've read here. Do the exercises. Think about what we've discussed. I wish I could make guarantees, but of course, that is impossible. What I can say is, if you put in the work, you will learn new things about yourself and learn about what it is you really want. I will be hoping and praying that you find the love that is waiting to be found.

CHAPTER TWENTY-SIX
He Said, She Said

I've said a number of times that while you are on your search for your needle in the haystack, someone else is searching for you. As you attack that pile of straw, as you sift through it and suffer the missteps and false starts on your journey, there is someone on the other side of that pile doing the same thing with the same hopes. As much joy as you may have in finding your needle, they will have just as much when finding theirs. To prove this to you, I thought you might like to hear the story of how my husband and I came together from *his* point of view. As truthful as I have tried to be in telling this tale, I think you'll see that a different perspective sometimes paints a different picture.

Fred D. Gooden

When Jameliah started this project, I did not expect to be asked to tell this story, but I get it. I'll tell you my side. Here we go.

My best friend, Kenya, and I have known each other for at least ten years, but I had never met her sister, Jameliah. Kenya encouraged us to meet, so we finally did. On February 22, we had our first conversation over video chat. From that one conversation, we continued to talk every day, all day. Every. Day.

It didn't matter where we were. I would be in my truck in Florida, and she would be at home in the Carolinas, and we would talk. In the evenings, we would talk until I fell asleep. We talked for hours and hours. This went on for at least three weeks. To be honest, it felt just like we were in school, and I was experiencing first love all over again. I was experiencing what first love *should* be.

The first time we actually met, she was attending a conference in Jacksonville, Florida. We made plans to meet at the conference and then get together afterward.

Now I knew she was a preacher. I am a preacher as well, and that was one of the ways in which we connected. It was exciting to meet someone who traveled in the same circles. So I knew she was a preacher, but I really didn't know she was a *preacher*.

I first laid eyes on her in person just before she was about to minister at this conference. Though we had spent so much time talking and video chatting, we had never been up close and personal. The first time we were in the same room, when she was right there, I saw her and ... I ran! I had been sitting near the front, but I scurried three rows back. I was overwhelmed. I thought, *Man, this is a powerful woman!*

I almost ran out of the room, but I thought, *You know what? I'm gonna take a chance.*

That night, we had our first date.

We were finally face to face. We were sharing the same space, the same air, and it was just awkward! I was in an awkward place, still feeling overwhelmed with realizing how powerful she was, not to mention the fact that I'm a divorcé, and at that point I hadn't been in the presence of another woman in a dating way since that experience. Jameliah was obviously tired after traveling and her role at the conference. Neither of us was in our best form, but it was crazy how awkward it was. It just did not go right. It was our first date, and it was horrible.

The next day, I went to work knowing the night had been a disaster. I felt how bad it was. I felt it in my chest. It was in my head; all day long, I kept thinking about how badly it had gone. I knew that I had fouled up my first date with the woman I wanted to be with.

WHEN WE FINALLY DID TALK LATER THAT DAY, SHE EXPRESSED ALL THE MISGIVINGS I THOUGHT SHE WOULD HAVE. SHE TOLD ME SHE DIDN'T THINK I WAS READY FOR A RELATIONSHIP. SHE SUGGESTED I NEEDED TO DATE OTHER PEOPLE FOR A WHILE.

I was crushed. I kept thinking, *Man, this lady here. I can't lose her.* We may have had a horrible first date … and it was horrible … but our time together on video calls, all the hours we'd talked—I knew we had something special. Every day she would send me a song. Every day I would send her one. We'd built such a great intimacy before we met, before we saw each other in person. I felt so close to her. Then, when we were finally face to face, able to actually touch each other and see each other, for it to go so wrong was completely crazy.

"WHEN YOU REALIZE YOU WANT TO SPEND THE REST OF YOUR LIFE WITH SOMEBODY, YOU WANT THE REST OF YOUR LIFE TO START AS SOON AS POSSIBLE."
—A LINE FROM THE MOVIE *WHEN HARRY MET SALLY*[68]

I kept thinking about it, and I blamed myself. I knew she had expected more from me. I knew she had been disappointed because … well, I was scared of her! I knew I hadn't handled it right.

Later, when we talked about the experience, she said I was wearing patent leather shoes and a church shirt. I realized the night had been so messed up, she couldn't even see me clearly because I had been wearing Nikes, jeans, and a casual shirt.

The day after the disaster of a date, I called a friend of mine, the one I call when I need to chew over something. I told him how badly I'd botched the date and told him what she had said. When he asked why I was so sure she was the one, I told him a story. I said that just a couple of days after the first time we talked, she called me while I was in my church in Jacksonville. She'd caught me just before I was about to go up to minister.

"Let me pray for you before you go up," she'd said.

She had no idea what that meant to me. No one had ever offered to do that for me. I'd never felt that type of support. I'd never felt that type of love. It just blew my mind. From that moment, I knew.

I told my friend this story and about our horrible date and that I felt I had messed it up. My friend told me he didn't see anything wrong, and he told me to just go for it.

So I called her and listened as she told me that I should date other people, that I wasn't ready. But I wouldn't give up. I talked her into letting me come see her one more time before she left town.

When that call ended, after she told me she would give it another shot, I swore I was going to make sure she wasn't going to get away from me. I knew. I knew she was my wife.

The last thing I wanted to do was be the corny guy who says, "The Lord told me you were going to be my wife." I didn't want to say that to her because, in our circle, we hear that kind of thing all the time. But from the first moment we started talking, from the first moment I saw a picture of her, I felt in my heart that she was my wife. Once she agreed to see me again and give me one last chance, I knew I had to make the most of it.

On our second date, I decided a different Fred was coming. This is the Fred who knew this special woman wasn't getting away from me. I had that determination in my head and in my heart. I'm telling you, I pulled out all the stops. I got as fresh as I could!

I went to the gym for a hard workout, and I bought some new shoes. I searched my closet and made sure I didn't wear anything churchy, and I put on my best cologne. This time, it was an afternoon date, and I had decided I was going to play her game.

I told her she was beautiful. I told her how surprised I was over her ministry. Then I told her I might take her suggestion and date other women for a while.

"I'm sitting right here," she said. "What are you talking about?"

At that point, I knew the tides had turned. I was able to pull it off and get my woman.

That first date? That first kiss? Nah. That was a disaster.

It was on the second date where she will tell you I came back with a vengeance.

Today I can say, without a shadow of a doubt, everything I saw from the beginning came true. And now she is Jameliah Gooden.

Book Club and Study Guide

At the beginning of this book, I suggested you share it with friends so you could have a circle of support and a way to discuss some of the issues and exercises along the way. It's one thing to read along, to mark the scriptures, and even to do the exercises provided for you at the end of chapters. It's a whole other thing to discuss the issues with other people who have read the same words and to gather those varying perspectives about what you've read. Experience is a great teacher. It's better to learn from the experience of others than to have to live those experiences yourself.

I'd like to suggest that you consider establishing Makeover Mondays, or really, whatever day of the week you'd like. Make it a goal to read a chapter a week, do the exercises, and then get together or meet in some kind of virtual meeting room. Discuss. Share. Learn.

Just to get you started, here are a few questions you can use to get the ideas flowing.

1. What is the value of listing out the characteristics you're looking for? Share your list with others and discuss. Are there things others have on their list that you might want to add to yours?
2. Describe your best and worst dating experiences. Why were they good? Why were they bad? More importantly, what did you learn from these experiences? Are there dating

mistakes you've made more than once? How can you ensure you won't make those same mistakes again? What types of data are you gathering while on a first date?

3. Self-value or self-worth is always something people have trouble accepting. Why do you think that is? Do you understand your own worth? Do you downplay your value to make yourself more approachable? Understanding your value could change your perspective on which characteristics are important to you on your list. Are you revisiting your list now with your own value in mind? Do the people in your discussion group agree that you've assessed your worth correctly?

4. We've learned that while we are searching the haystack, there is someone on the other side searching for us. What are the characteristics the person on the other side of the haystack might be searching for to find you? Do the people in your discussion group agree these are the characteristics you demonstrate?

5. In the past, have you settled for someone who did not meet the characteristics you have on your list? What was it about this person that made you decide to settle? Example: "They had lesser financial means than I wanted, but they were a good listener." What was the result of you making the compromise?

6. One of the exercises in the book is about self-sabotage. Discuss the ways in which you think you self-sabotage relationships. Does the group agree with your assessment? Is there one particular relationship that suffered from this self-sabotage? If so, what would you do differently?

7. As we mature, our list of things we would never consider in a partner grows shorter. Play this game. Go around the group and have each person finish this sentence: "I would never date someone who _____." As each person fills in the blank, others in the group should raise their hand if they agree. Discuss why there is agreement or disagreement.

Discuss whether there are things that once might have filled in the blank but are now acceptable to you.

8. We all present different faces in different situations. Are some of your faces more approachable than others? Do you think you need to work on your approachability? What do you think impacts your approachability? Are you approached by people with the characteristics you are looking for? Is there something you could change to attract the types of people you most want to meet?

9. Have you ever played matchmaker? What success, if any, have you had with matching people you know? Do you think there is value in having a matchmaker?

10. What do you think about using the nine fruits as indicators of The Real Thing? Name some ways you might identify each of the nine fruits: love, joy, peace, patience, kindness, goodness, faithfulness, gentleness, and self-control. Do you think the person who is searching the haystack for you would find the nine spirits in you? Are there people you have dated before who might deserve more consideration when using the nine spirits as a guide?

Acknowledgments

First, of course, I have to thank God for being the driving force in my good, my bad, and my different.

My mother, who always shows up—even in death. I always find encouragement in her memories because I've been taught that the body gets the grave but never gets the memories.

Of course, Dad, you are one of the reasons I had no choice but to be strong and brave. Even from the grave, you are still teaching me why I can't fail because of the strength you instilled in me as I lived in protection mode all those years in my childhood.

To my siblings, I love you all. I thank you for your support, your love, and your words of encouragement.

I thank my sisters Kenya, Joy and Michelle for the laughs at three in the morning. Thank you for allowing me to see how I can grow and mature by watching you all. Kenya is also a pastor, a special thank you to her for introducing me to the man God said I was supposed to be with, and thank you for allowing me to marry your best friend.

I have the most amazing children in the world. Dylan and Hunter, I thank you for showing me what my drive is about. It's about watching you smile and grow and mature. I always say, "Has Mommy ever let you down?" I work hard every day to make sure those words will never fall on deaf ears. I thank you for allowing me to be your mother. It is an honor to see your joy in each other.

It's even an honor to see you fight because, truth be told, it is in making up that we are able to continue and to learn the faults that keep us together as a family.

I would also like to thank Mindy Kuhn, Amy Ashby, Melissa Long, Mary Doyle and everyone at Warren Publishing who made this book possible.

I want to say thank you to Unity Charlotte International Church. You guys are part of my life and the audience God has ordained in the brick and mortar I can tangibly touch with my husband and my family. I thank you for being part of my life. We are a place of liberty, love, and laughter. We do that every Sunday. We do that every Wednesday. We do that whenever you see that light turning on, on Facebook. You have been part of my journey. You have seen me at my best and my worst and now, you see me at the height of joy that only God may have given. I want you to see my joy and be encouraged that if he did it for me, I know he will do it for you.

I need to say thank you to my assistant, Moe—I call her "Shell," or "My Freakin', Stinkin' Baby Sister"—thank you for keeping me in order. There is no one who can replace you.

To my friends, Eddie and Derikus, Gigi—my Glam Squad— Thank you so very much for being a part of my journey. I am so blessed to be rich, not in financial terms, but because I have people like you all who love me and are part of my journey every day. Please know that, every day, I would not be here, doing what I do, without such an amazing team.

While writing this book, one of the things I have to acknowledge is that I'd like to thank God for my mistakes. I thank God for giving me the courage to write those mistakes into the pages of this book. We never want to make mistakes, but because I've learned from them and learned to acknowledge that I have made mistakes, no one can judge me for them.

Before I jumped back into the rubble, I paused and got help. Through therapy, I learned what love is. I now know what love truly is. The Bible says I am sharper than iron. I found someone to help keep me sharp even while I made mistakes. Through God's grace, I was given a second chance at love because I faced my truth. Now I stand here, knowing what my mistakes were. Those mistakes are what prepared me for this journey with you, husband.

Fred D. Gooden III, you taught me what love is. You taught me patience. You introduced me to areas of my life I didn't know existed. You gave me a level of kindness I've never experienced in my entire life. You showed me who I could be and refused to accept what the world wanted me to be. You gave me laughter, unspeakable joy, and authentic love. In my life with you, you've showed me that it is easy to love everyone, and it is easy to give. But the most important thing you've taught me, Fred, is that it's easy to receive. The road to you was a long, painful, treacherous path. A path where so much was taken from me. God saw fit to save my life. You were the one who came along and fixed what others had broken, and you gave me what others could never provide.

Together, we have a family of eight children, and each one has given me a different level of happy. We are a huge family, and we thrive in that.

You gave me a mother in Adell Brown, who provides me with the touch and a kind word from a mother who I have not heard from in years.

My life experience was with men who used, abused, and took. Men who walked away with everything I worked so hard for. You came and repaired and healed and restored me. Fred, you have carried the pain others caused and allowed me to love freely without a false face. You taught me what it is to miss someone, even when they're just in another room. You taught me that the laughter I lost in writing my last book can come back so genuinely that it infects others around us. Our joy is infectious.

Fred, will you be my husband forever? Will you be my friend until the angels call our name? I want to build a legacy with you, beyond this book, beyond the church. When I become old, with a headful of gray hair and no teeth, I want to look over and see you as beautiful as you are now.

Only God can do this. I seal this acknowledgment with the promise that I will never let you or our family down.

The Car Chronicles
Movement Family

Every morning at 7:30 a.m. (EST), live on Facebook, The Car Chronicles Movement family gathers together to share our faith. We share good times and bad. We sometimes come together as a family. Sometimes we fight together when we get interlopers from Facebook who aren't familiar with the strength of our movement.

I want to send a special thank you to the Car Chronicles Movement family for your clicks, tags, shares, and watch parties. You are so faithful. You are there every morning. I thank you because as much as you may think I encourage you, you encourage me. Days when I want to give up, you are there for me. You ping me in my inbox, asking, "Where's the crazy lady in the car?"

About the Author

Pastor Jamelia Gooden is the daughter of the late Evangelist Violetta B. Young and Pastor James I. Young and grew up in Brooklyn, New York, as the youngest of four kids. At the tender age of nine, Jameliah's mother predicted that she would carry the gospel. At age thirteen, Jameliah delivered her first sermon at Kingsborough Community College in Brooklyn. She then began to speak at local churches in New Jersey under the leadership of the late Reverend Ronald B. Christian. Since then, she has preached across the United States and internationally and is the Pastor of Unity Charlotte International. Jameliah is an experienced keynote speaker for women's empowerment, teen and youth mentoring, Corporate America, and relationships. She is the voice behind the popular Car Chronicles Movement, where she can be seen live on Facebook Monday through Friday at 7:30 a.m. (EST).

Jameliah is the proud mother of a son and daughter. Together, with her husband, Fred D. Gooden, also a pastor, they have a blended family of eight children. They live in Charlotte, North Carolina.

Jameliah is the author of the best-selling book, *The Death of the Angry Black Woman* (Warren Publishing, 2018).

To learn more about the Car Chronicles Movement (CCM), visit https://www.carchronicles.org/.

All are welcome to join CCM on Facebook at https://www.facebook.com/jameliah2/.

Learn all about CCM and the Jameliah Gooden ministry on YouTube at https://www.youtube.com/c/PastorJameliah.

And follow Jameliah on Instagram at https://www.instagram.com/car_chronicles_movement/.

Endnotes

1 "A Needle in a Haystack," Merriam-Webster.com Dictionary, Merriam-Webster, accessed July 15, 2021, https://www.merriam-webster.com/dictionary/a%20needle%20in%20a%20haystack.

2 Miguel de Cervantes, *Don Quixote de la Mancha* (New York: Modern Library, 1998).

3 "Heaps," Edpresso, Educative.io, accessed July 15, 2021, https://www.educative.io/edpresso/what-is-a-heap.

4 Yerís H. Mayol-García, Benjamin Gurrentz, and Rose M. Kreider, "Number, Timing, and Duration of Marriages and Divorces: 2016," *Current Population Reports,* U.S. Census Bureau, Washington, DC, 2021, 70–167.

5 Slyvia Plath, *The Bell Jar* (New York: Harper Perennial Modern Classics, 2006).

6 "Ruby," Merriam-Webster.com Dictionary, Merriam-Webster, accessed July 17, 2021, https://www.merriam-webster.com/dictionary/ruby.

7 Proverbs 31:10 (English Standard Version, 2011).

8 Elisa Lipsky-Karasz, "Beyoncé's Baby Love," *Harper's Bazaar,* October 11, 2011, accessed July 15, 2021, https://www.harpersbazaar.com/celebrity/latest/news/a825/beyonces-baby-love-interview-1111/.

9 "Study: Dating and Relationship Statistics," Match.com, Match Group, February 4, 2011, accessed July 17, 2021, https://www.match.com/2011-relationship-dating-statistics.

10 "Discovery," Merriam-Webster.com Dictionary, Merriam-Webster, accessed July 15, 2021, https://www.merriam-webster.com/dictionary/discovery.

11 "The Dating Game (1965–1986)," IMDb, accessed July 20, 2021, https://www.imdb.com/title/tt0058795/.

12 "Somewhere Out There," by James Horner, Barry Mann, and Cynthis Weil, as performed by Betsy Cathcart and Phillip Glasser, *An American Tail*, MCA Records, 1986.

13 "Online Dating Statistics: 60% of Users Look for Long Term Relationships," ReportLinker.com, February 9, 2017, accessed March 29, 2021, ReportLinker.com/insight/finding-love-online.html.

14 Korin Miller, "The Pitfalls of Dating: How to Tell What to Do About It," *Women's Health Magazine*, February 6, 2017, accessed June, 2021, https://www.womenshealthmag.com/relationships/a19946959/addiction-to-dating/.

15 —, "Pitfalls of Dating."

16 Maya Angelou, "When Someone Shows You Who You Are, Believe Them," Oprah.com, Oprah Life Class, featuring Oprah Winfrey, aired October 26, 2011, accessed July 21, 2021, https://www.oprah.com/oprahs-lifeclass/when-people-show-you-who-they-are-believe-them-video.

17 "A Dating Renaissance," Singles in America, Match.com, accessed June 3, 2021, https://www.singlesinamerica.com/a-dating-renaissance.

18 Ecclesiastes 4:9–12 (English Standard Version, 2011).

19 "Settle," Merriam-Webster.com Dictionary, Merriam-Webster, accessed July 17, 2021, https://www.merriam-webster.com/dictionary/settle.

20 Gwendolyn Seidman, PhD, "5 Essential Qualities for a Romantic Partner," *Psychology Today*, February 25, 2017, accessed June 5, 2021, https://www.psychologytoday.com/us/blog/close-encounters/201702/5-essential-qualities-romantic-partner.

21 "Red-flag," Merriam-Webster.com Dictionary, Merriam-Webster, accessed July 17, 2021, https://www.merriam-webster.com/dictionary/red-flag.

22 Rossana Snee, "11 Red Flags in a Relationship Not to Ignore," LifeHack.org, February, 24, 2021, accessed June 5, 2021, https://www.lifehack.org/375731/50-red-flags-you-should-watch-for-your-relationship.

23 Alice Walker, *The Color Purple* (New York: Open Road Media, 2011), Amazon Kindle, 39.

24 "Population: Black Male Statistics," BlackDemographics.com, accessed June 5, 2021, https://blackdemographics.com/population/black-male-statistics/.

25 Isaiah 4:1 (English Standard Version, 2011).

26 "Annual Estimates of the Resident Population by Sex, Age, Race Alone or in Combination, and Hispanic Origin for the United States: April 1, 2010 to July 1, 2019," 2019 Population Estimates by Age, Sex, Race, and Hispanic Origin, U.S. Census Bureau, June 25, 2020, accessed July 20, 2021, https://www.census.gov/newsroom/press-kits/2020/population-estimates-detailed.html.

27 Dianne M. Stewart, "2019 Marked 400 Years of 'Forbidden Black Love' in America," *The Washington Post*, December 26, 2019, accessed July 22, 2021, https://www.washingtonpost.com/outlook/2019/12/26/marked-years-forbidden-black-love-america/.

28 Rose M. Kreider and Renee Ellis, "Number, Timing, and Duration of Marriages and Divorces: 2009," May 2011, accessed July 21, 2021, https://www.census.gov/prod/2011pubs/p70-125.pdf.

29 "Budget," Merriam-Webster.com Dictionary, Merriam-Webster, accessed July 17, 2021, https://www.merriam-webster.com/dictionary/budget.

30 "Approachable," Merriam-Webster.com Dictionary, Merriam-Webster, accessed July 17, 2021, https://www.merriam-webster.com/dictionary/approachable.

31 Irma Thomas, vocalist, "Time Is On My Side," by Jerry Ragovoy (Norman Meade), track B1 on *Wish Someone Would Care*, Capitol Records, 1964.

32 Ecclesiastes 3:1, 3:8 (English Standard Version, 2011).

33 "Bridebook.co.uk Marriage Report, 2017," Bridebook.co.uk, accessed July 17, 2021, https://bridebook.com/uk/article/bridebook-co-uk-marriage-report-2017.

34 "Divorces in England and Wales: 2019," Office of National Statistics, accessed July 17, 2021, https://www.ons.gov.uk/peoplepopulationandcommunity/birthsdeathsandmarriages/divorce/bulletins/divorcesinenglandandwales/2019.

35 Joshua J. Mark, "Heraclitus of Ephesos," *World History Encyclopedia*, Unesco Archives, July 14, 2010, accessed July 17, 2021, https://www.worldhistory.org/Heraclitus_of_Ephesos/.

36 "Wait," Merriam-Webster.com Dictionary, Merriam-Webster, accessed July 17, 2021, https://www.merriam-webster.com/dictionary/wait.

37 1 Corinthians 7:34 (English Standard Version, 2011).

38 ——, (English Standard Version, 2011).

39 "Extreme Cheapskates (2011–2014)," IMDb, accessed July 20, 2021, https://www.imdb.com/title/tt2152721/.

40 Kevin Thompson, "Do People Get Their Ex Back? If Yes, Do

They Stay Together? If Not, Do They Move On? An In-Depth Study," Ex Back Permanently, accessed June 7, 2021, https://exbackpermanently.com/do-people-get-their-ex-back-study/.

41 Proverbs 26:11 (English Standard Version, 2011).

42 The Relentless Conservative, "Something We Might Agree On: Beauty?" Huffington Post, Buzzfeed, Inc., last updated October 22, 2011, accessed on July 21, 2021, https://www.huffpost.com/entry/something-we-might-agree-_b_932870.

43 James Baldwin, *The Fire Next Time* (New York: Penguin Classics, 1990).

44 "Type," Merriam-Webster.com Dictionary, Merriam-Webster, accessed July 17, 2021, https://www.merriam-webster.com/dictionary/type.

45 Psalm 37:4 (English Standard Version, 2011).

46 "Sapiosexual," Merriam-Webster.com Dictionary, Merriam-Webster, accessed July 17, 2021, https://www.merriam-webster.com/dictionary/sapiosexual.

47 Yehuda Berg, "The Power of Words," Huffington Post, Buzzfeed, Inc, last updated November 17, 2011, accessed July 17, 2021, https://www.huffpost.com/entry/the-power-of-words_1_b_716183.

48 2 Corinthians 4:16 (English Standard Version, 2011).

49 Proverbs 4:7 (English Standard Version, 2011).

50 Psalm 140:3 (English Standard Version, 2011).

51 James 3:5, 7–8, (English Standard Version, 2011).

52 William Shakespeare, *Love's Labour's Lost: The Oxford Shakespeare* (Oxford: Oxford University Press, 2008), 2.1.13–16.

53 "Bublé Needed Therapy After Blunt Split," Express, November 1, 2009, accessed July 17, 2021, https://www.express.co.uk/celebrity-news/137534/Buble-needed-therapy-after-Blunt-split.

54 "Suspicious Minds," by Mark James, as performed by Elvis Presley, *From Elvis in Memphis,* Sony Music Entertainment, 1969.

55 "Ghosting," Merriam-Webster.com Dictionary, Merriam-Webster, accessed July 17, 2021, https://www.merriam-webster.com/dictionary/ghosting.

56 Darlene Lancer, JD, MFT, "8 Reasons You've Been Ghosted," PsychCentral.com, August 4, 2019, accessed July 18, 2021, https://psychcentral.com/lib/8-reasons-youve-been-ghosted#5.

57 "Fatal Attraction," IMDb, accessed July 18, 2021, https://www.imdb.com/title/tt0093010/plotsummary#synopsis.

58 Lancer, PsychCentral.com. 4.3.78–79.

59 William Shakespeare, *The Taming of the Shrew: Folger Shakespeare Library* (New York: Simon and Schuster, 2004)

60 Eduardo Angel Visuals, "Joshua Bell and the Washington Post Subway Experiment," YouTube, January 25, 2012, https://www.youtube.com/watch?v=LZeSZFYCNRw.

61 Kelly Rudnicki, "Finding Success Through Failure," PBS Food Home, July 29, 2012, accessed July 18, 2021, https://www.pbs.org/food/julia-child-100-birthday-cookforjulia/finding-success-through-failure/.

62 Fred Hutchinson, "Men Leave: Separation And Divorce Far More Common When The Wife Is The Patient" Science Daily, Cancer Research Center, November 10, 2009, accessed June 10, 2021, https://www.sciencedaily.com/releases/2009/11/091110105401.htm.

63 "Counterfeit," Merriam-Webster.com Dictionary, Merriam-Webster, accessed July 18, 2021, https://www.merriam-webster.com/dictionary/counterfeit.

64 "Ain't Nothing Like the Real Thing," by Nicholas Ashford and Valerie Simpson, as performed by Marvin Gaye and Tammi Terrell, *You're All I Need,* Motown Records, 1968.

65 1 John 4:18 (English Standard Version, 2011).

66 Ecclesiastes 10:10 (English Standard Version, 2011).

67 Galatians 5:16–23 (English Standard Version, 2011).

68 *When Harry Met Sally*, directed by Rob Reiner (1989; Castle Rock Entertainment and Nelson Entertainment).

Bibliography

Angelou, Maya. "When Someone Shows You Who You Are, Believe Them." Oprah.com. Oprah Life Class. Featuring Oprah Winfrey. Aired October 26, 2011. Accessed July 21, 2021. https://www.oprah.com/oprahs-lifeclass/when-people-show-you-who-they-are-believe-them-video.

Baldwin, James. *The Fire Next Time.* New York: Penguin Classics, 1990.

Berg, Yehuda. "The Power of Words." Huffington Post. Buzzfeed, Inc. Last updated November 17, 2011. Accessed July 17, 2021. https://www.huffpost.com/entry/the-power-of-words_1_b_716183.

Betsy Cathcart and Phillip Glasser, performers. "Somewhere Out There." Lyrics by James Horner, Barry Mann, and Cynthis Weil. *An American Tail.* MCA Records, 1986.

Bridebook.co.uk. "Bridebook.co.uk Marriage Report, 2017." Accessed July 17, 2021. https://bridebook.com/uk/article/bridebook-co-uk-marriage-report-2017.

BlackDemographics.com. "Population: Black Male Statistics." Accessed June 5, 2021. https://blackdemographics.com/population/ black-male-statistics/.

"Bublé Needed Therapy After Blunt Split." Express. November 1, 2009. Accessed July 17, 2021. https://www.express.co.uk/celebrity-news/137534/Buble-needed-therapy-after-Blunt-split.

de Cervantes, Miguel. *Don Quixote de la Mancha*. New York: Modern Library, 1998.

Edpresso. "Heaps." Educative.io. Accessed July 15, 2021. https:// www.educative.io/edpresso/what-is-a-heap.

Eduardo Angel Visuals. "Joshua Bell and the Washington Post Subway Experiment." YouTube. January 25, 2012. https://www. youtube.com/watch?v=LZeSZFYCNRw.

Gaye, Marvin and Tammi Terrell, performers. "Ain't Nothing Like the Real Thing." Lyrics by Nicholas Ashford and Valerie Simpson. *You're All I Need*. Motown Records, 1968.

GO TO LIST

Make a list of standards (a mandatory list that does not change) and a list of those things you can settle with (things that are not deal breakers).

Standards

Examples:
You must have a job

Settling
(Red-Flag list)

You must be six foot tall (your ideal person could be five feet eight inches tall).

Have fun fellowshiping on your search.

CPSIA information can be obtained
at www.ICGtesting.com
Printed in the USA
BVHW030153131121
621485BV00003B/81

9 781954 614727